I0800499

VOICES OF AMERICA

GADSDEN

Stories of the Great Depression

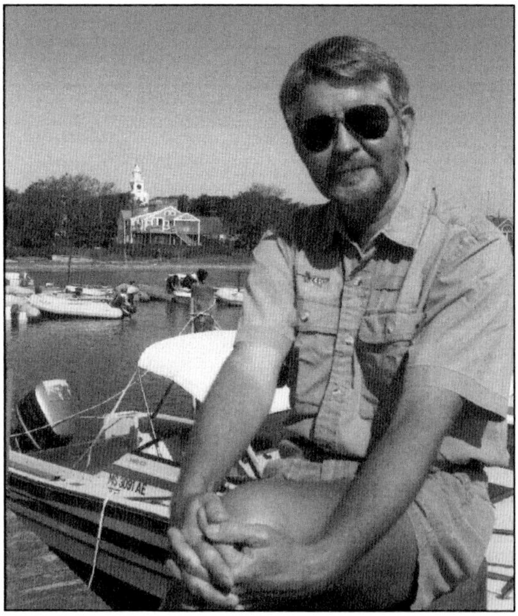

Robert Wilbanks holds a BA in Journalism and an MA in Film Communication from the University of Alabama. His photographs and articles have appeared in magazines and newspapers throughout the country. Wilbanks is the author of *Through the Eyes of a Parrot*, a collection of short stories set in the Caribbean.

Author's Note

Having grown up in Alabama, I always had a natural curiosity about the history of the South. It is undeniable that the South wears a distinctive game face unique to no other region of the country. It has its own language, politics, religion; it moves slowly to its own rhythm and pulse, in sync with its own history and sense of well-being in relation to the country and world at large.

Today, for many reasons, this distinctiveness is beginning to fade and, in some cases, disappear entirely. It is my purpose here to try to capture a few attributes of the South.

Initially, my father approached me with the idea for this book almost 30 years ago. During those years, he was employed full-time with his job and I was working at a newspaper as a photographer and feature writer. Since then he has retired and I've published numerous magazine articles, as well as a book of short stories.

When he had a birthday recently, and entered his eighth decade of life, he once again felt the time was right for the story to be told, to finally demand its own voice.

My father, Paul Wilbanks, was born in 1920, nine years before the start of the Great Depression. Like everyone who survived this horrible economic epoch, those years left a permanent impression on his life.

So this book, then, is his story. It is the story of his youth in the South and the way things were for him, between the years of 1930 and 1940—the years of the Great Depression.

—Robert Wilbanks

VOICES OF AMERICA

GADSDEN

Stories of the Great Depression

Robert Wilbanks

ARCADIA
PUBLISHING

ISBN 978-0-7385-0348-6

Published by Arcadia Publishing
Charleston, South Carolina

Printed in the United States of America

Library of Congress Catalog Card Number: Applied for

For all general information contact Arcadia Publishing at:
Telephone 843-853-2070
Fax 843-853-0044
E-Mail sales@arcadiapublishing.com
For customer service and orders:
Toll-Free 1-888-313-2665

Visit us on the Internet at www.arcadiapublishing.com

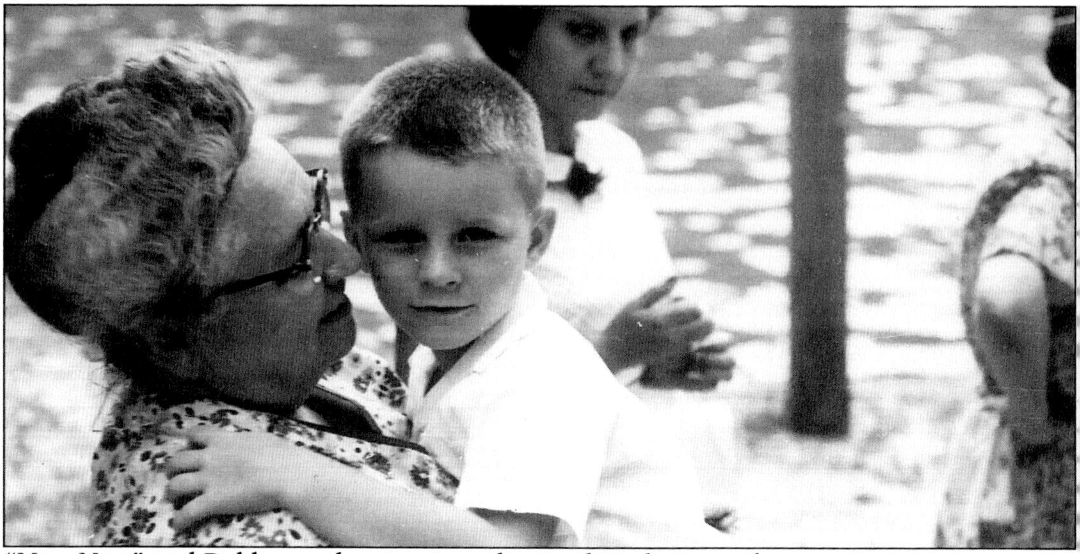

"Maw-Maw" and Bobby can be seen together in this photograph.

Dedication

For Minnie Lee Wilbanks (1895-1983): a wife, mother and grandmother who gave tirelessly with no calculation of recompense, yet who administered love, kindness and discipline with a measure of devotion known only to God.

"The past is never dead. It's not even past."

—Gavin Stevens,
Intruder in the Dust

Contents

Author's Note		2
Introduction		6
Acknowledgements		6
1.	The Good Old Days	7
2.	The Winter of Despair	11
3.	WPA	17
4.	Unions	21
5.	Politics	23
6.	Institution of Higher Learning	25
7.	Grocery Store	27
8.	Mini-business District	33
9.	Peddlers and Curb Markets	35
10.	The Home Place	37
11.	The Kitchen	39
12.	Depression Food	43
13.	Wash Day	45
14.	Milk	47
15.	The Family	49
16.	Church	51
17.	Christmas	55
18.	A Doctor's Visit	57
19.	Family Garden	59
20.	Our Cars	61
21.	Automobiles	63
22.	Telephones	67
23.	Radio	69
24.	Schools	71
25.	Getting a Job	75
26.	Entertainment	77
27.	Sports	83
28.	Visiting in the Country	87
29.	Making Sorghum	93
Conclusion		95
End Notes		96

Introduction

The era of the 1930s, the period of the Great Depression, was very influential on my life. For whatever reason, I have more memories of those years than of any other time. Though living conditions were hard, it did not take a lot to entertain us.

Those Depression years were an era when neighbors, though suffering in their own way, were really "neighborly." If a person had a problem, it became a problem for the entire community. This closeness, the unity of an entire neighborhood, was an asset that is sorely missed today.

Such "neighborliness" was destroyed by the automobile, television, and air-conditioning. Without these modern conveniences, people sat on their front porches and visited, exchanging news.

When automobiles and air-conditioning became common, things changed; people were either on the go or they stayed inside—where it was warm in winter, cool in summer, and they had a television to entertain them year-round.

This community spirit is no doubt the biggest loss to society at large and has led to the sense of isolation that permeates our modern day world.

In 1930, my grandfather—on my mother's side—died and we moved in with my grandmother. We lived with her, in her house, the entire decade of the 1930s. Upon her death in 1940, we moved into our own home.

In 1930, I was 10 years old and still in grammar school. During the next decade, between 1930 and 1940, I went from grammar school to high school; at the end of that period I started college.

Though the years were hard and difficult, I look back on the decade of the 1930s as the happiest and most fulfilling time in life. In the stories that follow, I hope to share some of those good times and old memories with you.

—Paul Wilbanks

Acknowledgments

The author wishes to acknowledge the kind cooperation of Mr. Bob Scarboro, who permitted photographs from his historic collection to be reprinted in this book. Special thanks to Mary Ella Wilbanks for her help in proofreading the manuscript.

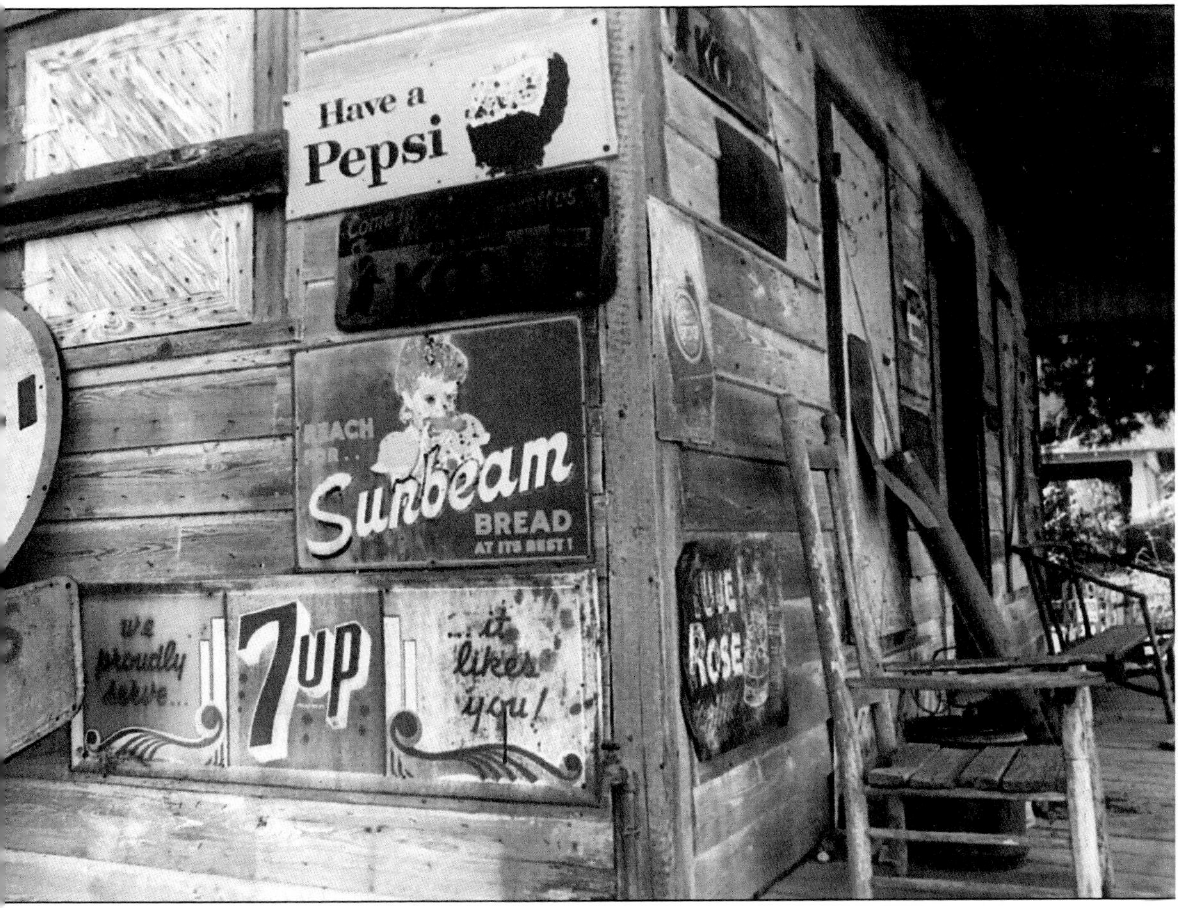

During the 1930s, the outside of a country store was usually decorated with advertisements for products available inside.

THE GOOD OLD DAYS

Today, with the uncertainty that exists in our modern world, Americans are longingly looking back at a period in rural America which was lived at a slower pace.

Simple taste. Simple pleasure. Life in the "good old days" of the 1930s was a time of extreme hardship, but it was also a time when a person could experience real personal satisfaction in the simple chores of life.

During this era, the economy of the South was basically one of agriculture and the majority of people lived on a family farm, known as "the old homeplace."

The rural family was almost a self-sufficient unit. Each farm had a garden, provided its own milk and eggs, raised meat, and grew feed for the stock.

During the season, the vegetables for the winter were canned; "Old Bossie" daily provided the milk needs while ham, sausage, and lard came from the "fattened hog."

All the necessities could not be provided on the farm. A cash crop, usually cotton, was raised, which enabled the farmer to make purchases that were absolutely necessary.

For most families, these purchases were made at a general store. In early rural America, with its scattered farmhouses, it was the country store that brought

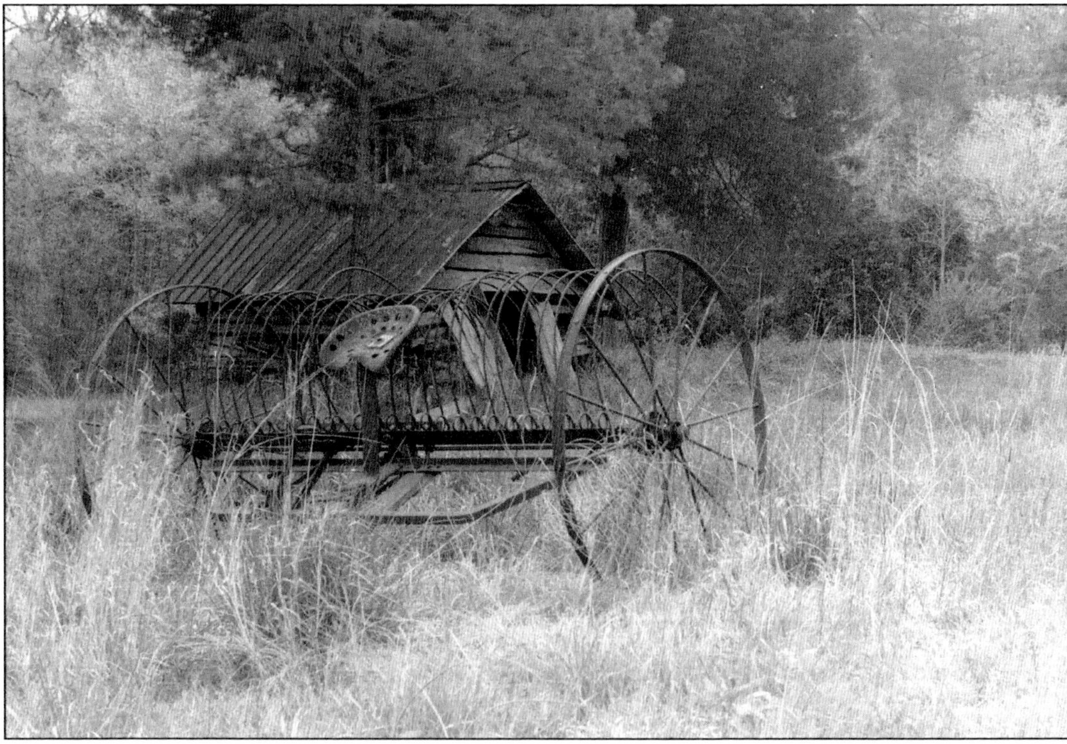

A hay rake sits idle until harvest.

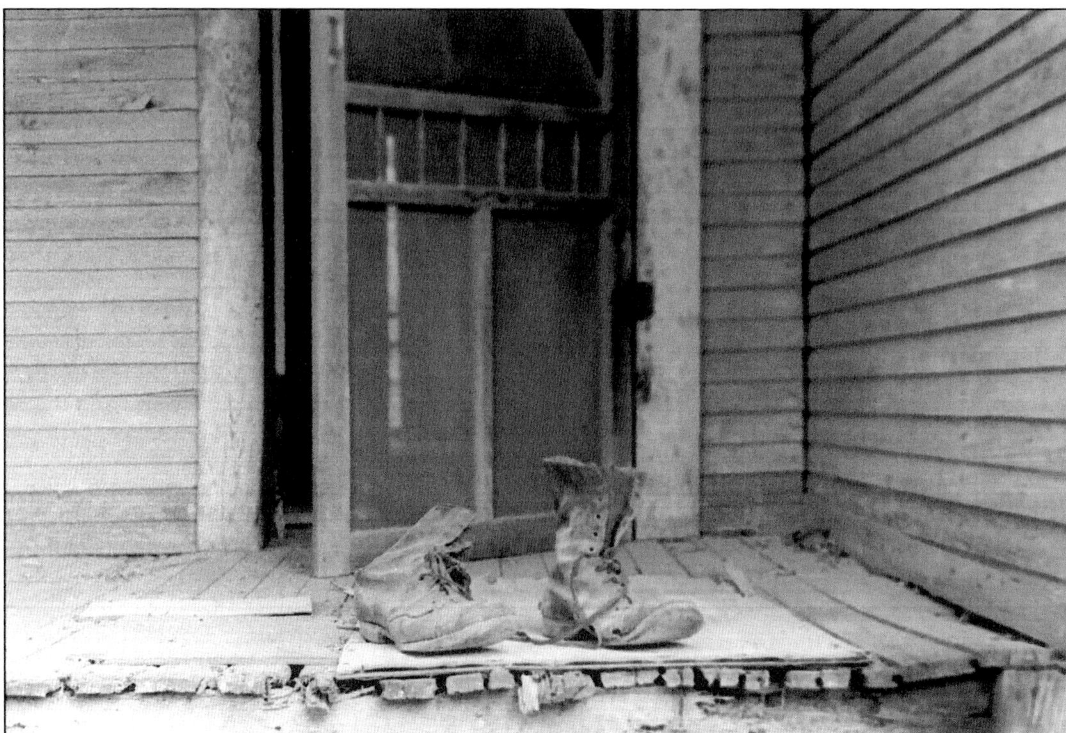

The boots represent the end of a hard day's work on the farm.

together a community. The store at the dusty crossroads made a neighborhood out of these houses and gave the area a personality of its own.

A visit to a country store was looked upon as a cherished treat. The trips were made sparingly and then only out of necessity. The store sold everything from candy to clothes and from medicine to farm implements. The most basic items sold were sugar, salt, coffee, and flour; the youngsters favored candy jawbreakers, orange slices, peppermint sticks, and peanut brittle.

In the fall, the cotton was sold and the farmer received his pay for a year's work. This money was used to buy clothes for his family, kerosene for the lamps, and groceries such as flour and salt.

Work on the farm changed with each season. Spring was the time when borrowing money was usually necessary to make a new crop; time was spent in preparing the land and, finally, planting the crop. Early summer meant hot, continuous field work until the crop was "laid by." After this, the family was given more free hours—chances to attend "protracted" meetings (all day singing with dinner on the ground), the big Fourth of July picnics with tubs of pink lemonade, and time to loaf at their favorite swimming hole.

Then, before organized swimming in concrete pools was known, young boys would either skinny-dip in a nearby creek or swim wearing a pair of cut-off overalls. After their swim, they would change back into dry street clothes and leave the wet overalls on the bank for someone else to use; or until next time, when they were able to sneak away for a quick dip.

With the arrival of fall, the tempo again picked up. Cotton had to be picked, corn gathered, and sorghum made—all in preparation for the coming winter months. The winter brought more activities into the house.

For the women, this was a time of social gatherings and quilting; the men spent

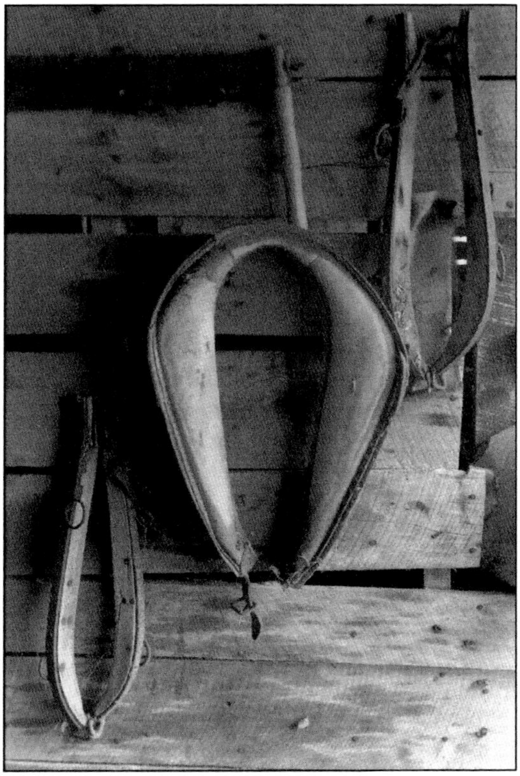

A horse collar hangs on the barn wall.

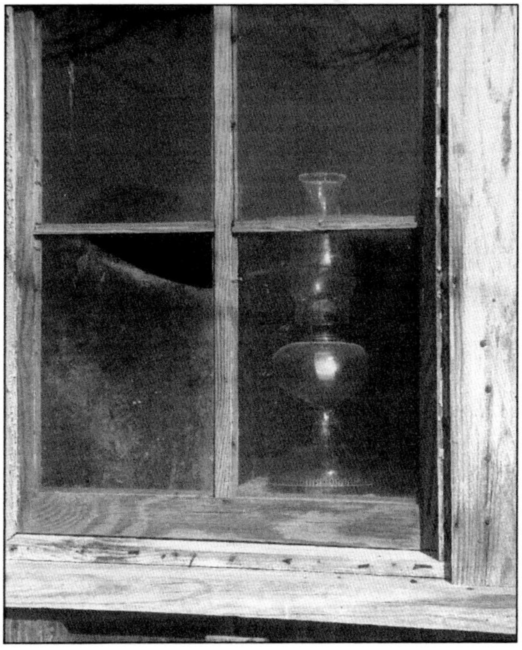

A light in the window of an old farmhouse was always a welcomed sight to friends and family.

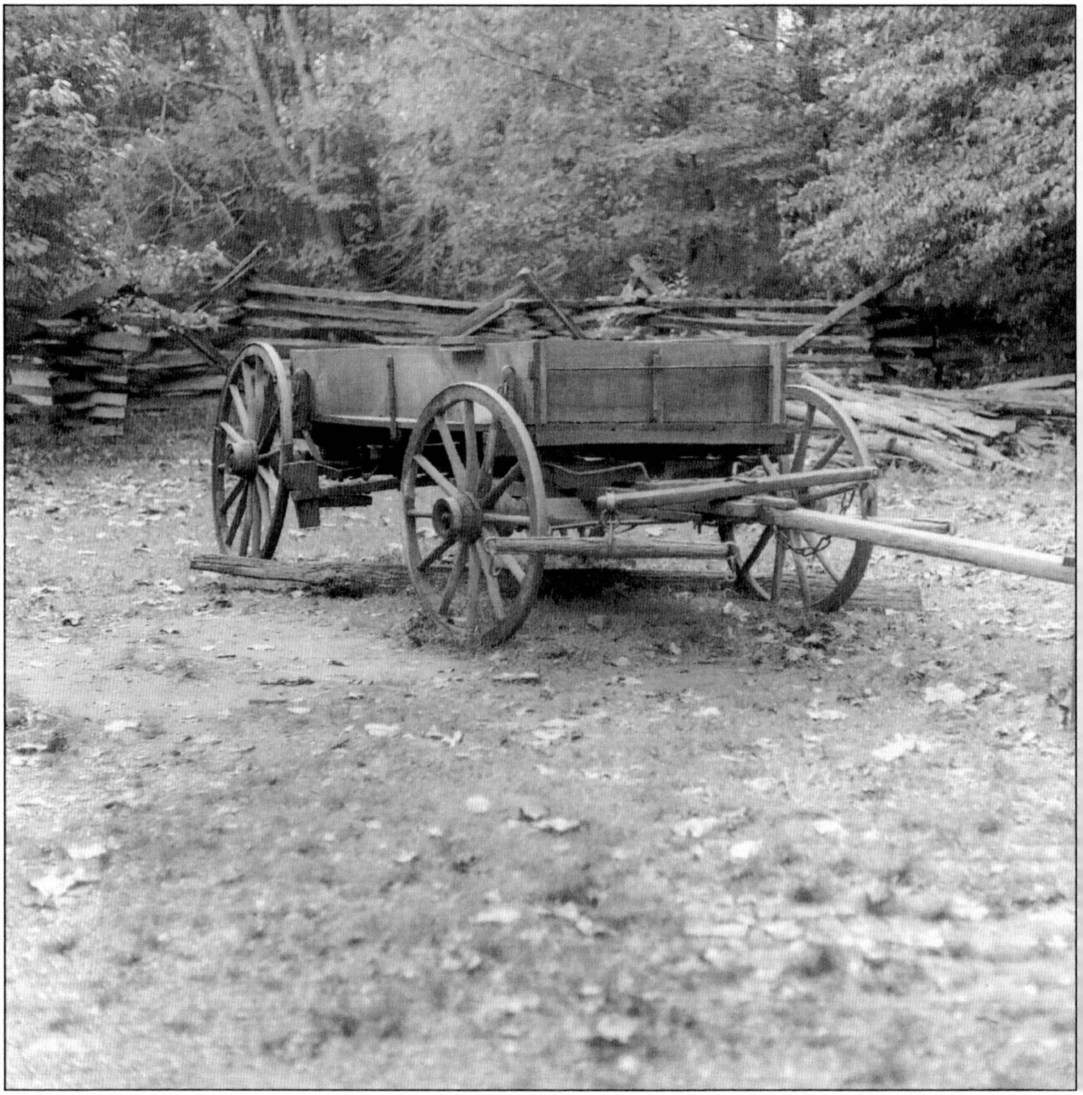

The farm wagon was used to transport farm produce to market and to attend social functions.

their free time with "Old Blue," hunting rabbits and squirrels.

With the Great Depression and, in close succession, World War II, that known world changed rapidly. New lifestyles, new ideas, and new types of machinery all helped pave the road to financial success and an easier life of which so many had always dreamed.

But these same benefits, sadly, opened the doors of uncertainty that are still swinging freely. Although no one in the South would trade the modern conveniences of today for the hardships of this earlier era, there is much to be said for the day when people were content with the simple things of life.

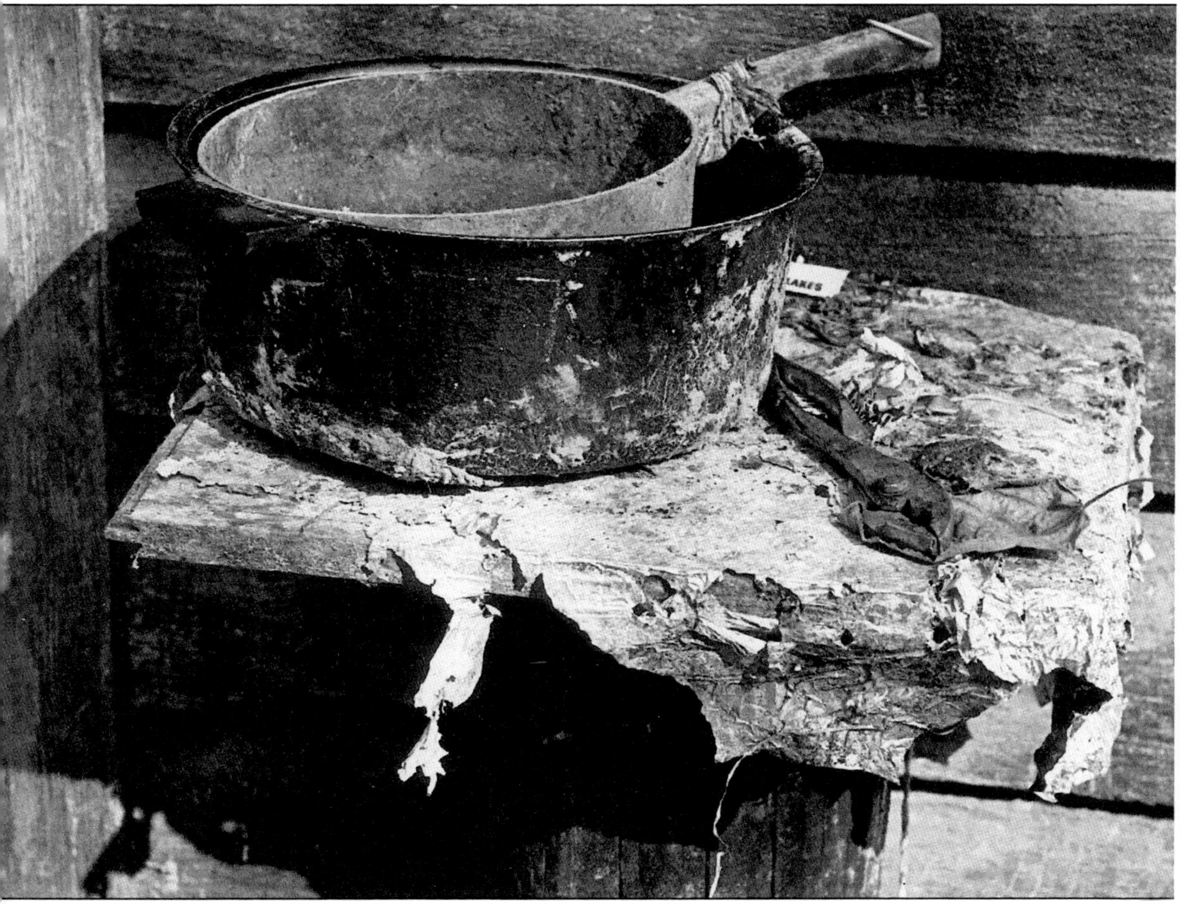

Empty pots and pans reflect the hopeless conditions of the 1930s for the many families who struggled to survive.

The Winter of Despair: An Overview of the Depression Years

The 1930s were an unparalleled period in American history. Never before or since—and probably never again—has the gamut of human emotions swung so far, so fast.

Herbert Hoover ushered in the new decade as the president of a prosperous nation. A nation whose mood was set—"it wanted to enjoy in peace the multitude of goods and gadgets it had discovered its modern, efficient industrial plants could produce in ever greater quantities."[1]

Big business was being crowned King. Automobiles were providing for a "mobile society." Extensive radio broadcasting was taking place. There was a rebirth in the arts and literature. Providing a backdrop for all this activity was prohibition, taking both the time and effort of everyone on both sides of the issue. Such was the atmosphere and conditions prevailing in America before "The Great Crash."

On October 29, 1929, the stock market crashed and soon after, the nation of plenty was in turmoil and fast becoming a wasteland. No sacred institution was left untouched; banks failed, factories shut

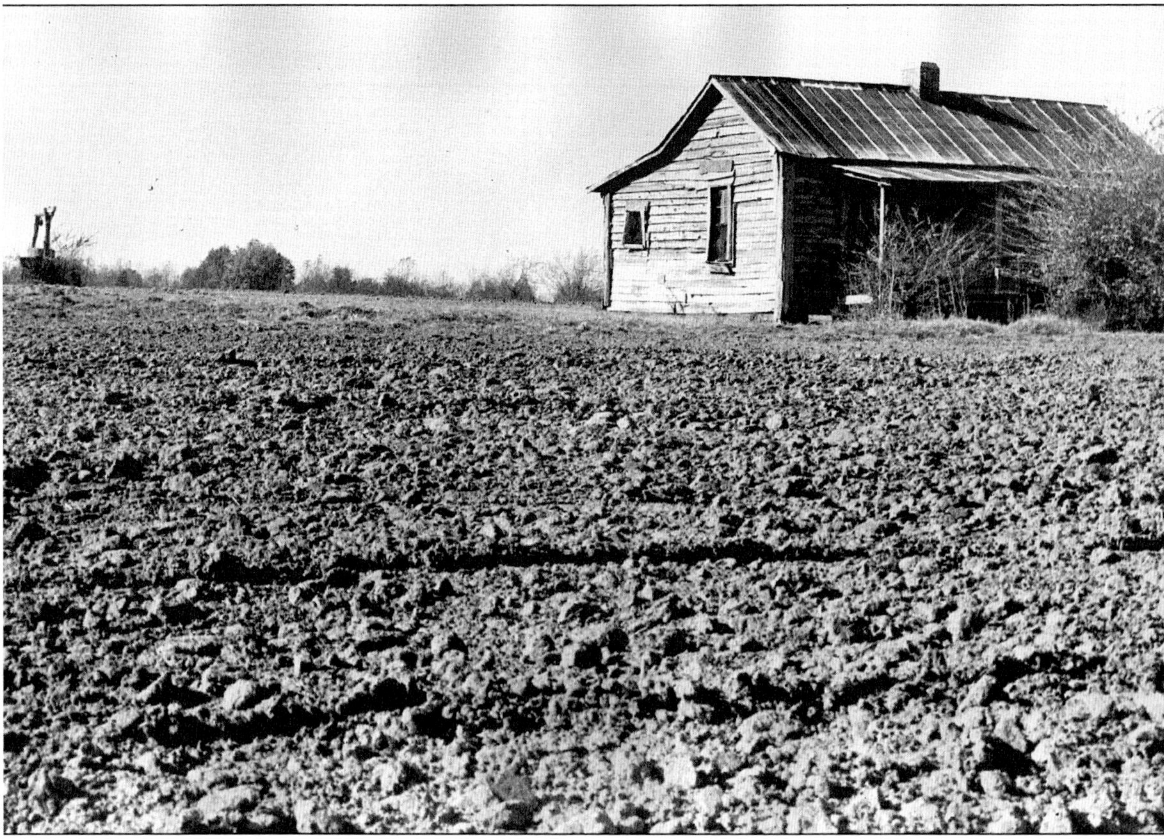

A deserted farmhouse is the only reminder of a once-prosperous farm operation during the hard economic years of the Depression.

down, stores closed, and almost every business seemed paralyzed.

Foreign trade screeched to a standstill. The national income dwindled from 81 billion dollars in 1929 to less than 68 billion in 1930, and hit bottom in 1932 with 41 billion.

The country was swiftly becoming a nation of the unemployed. In 1930, slightly more than three million employables were out of work; before the end of that year, the figure reached 10 million. The per capita yearly income (adjusted to the cost of living) tumbled from $681 in 1929 to $495 in 1933.[2]

Some people, determined to find a job, kept trudging from factory to factory and held a small hope that someday, there would again be a job for them. Many reverted to apathy, unable to find a job and defeated by a condition they couldn't fight.

"There are even stories of men who left their homes as usual each morning and returned each evening, traveling as they previously had, even though they no longer had an office to go to. When Soviet Russia announced there were available in that country jobs for 6,000 skilled workers, over 100,000 Americans applied." [3]

Men begged to serve on juries instead of trying to avoid their civic duty as once they had done because it paid comparatively well. Hundreds of males of all ages—from boys to old men—in large cities took up shoe shining at a time when fewer people could afford shoeshines, even at the cut-rate price of five cents.

In every unemployed person, there existed a great collapse of the spirit. Many clergy and social workers reported, with increasing distress, on the effect the Depression had upon family life. The father of the family, proud to be a good provider, was now often the dependent of his children and wife. With such conditions as these, many thousands of men and women took to the road.

In increasing numbers, "hobo jungles" and "Hoovervilles" became a common sight on the outskirts of most towns. Whole families moved on in a vague search for a better place to live or simply because they had no other place to go.

When Franklin D. Roosevelt was elected president the federal government began a construction program for roads and public buildings, and created several government agencies to provide jobs for the unemployed.

With the establishment of government agencies such as the Workers' Progress Administration (WPA) and the Civilian Conservation Core (CCC), conditions improved slightly for some of the unemployed. Both agencies were set up to train and to work for needy persons. The WPA provided jobs in public works projects, such as building roads, while the CCC hired unemployed young men for conservation work.

While the unemployment rate was rising constantly, the farm situation was also becoming worse as wholesale prices for food products went downhill rapidly. The prices the farmer received went downhill so rapidly, that between 1929 and 1932 net farm income dropped to less than one-third of what it had been. One problem was that the farmer's taxes and debts, especially the farm mortgages, remained at the high level of the 1920s.

When the Depression struck the cities of America in late 1929, it brought no startling news to the farmer. Rural people in large sections were hardly aware of a

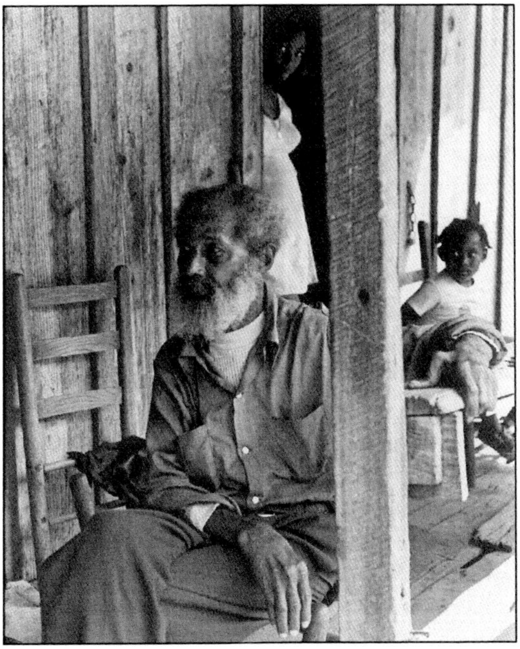

Whole families were affected by the Depression, but worked together to survive the hard times.

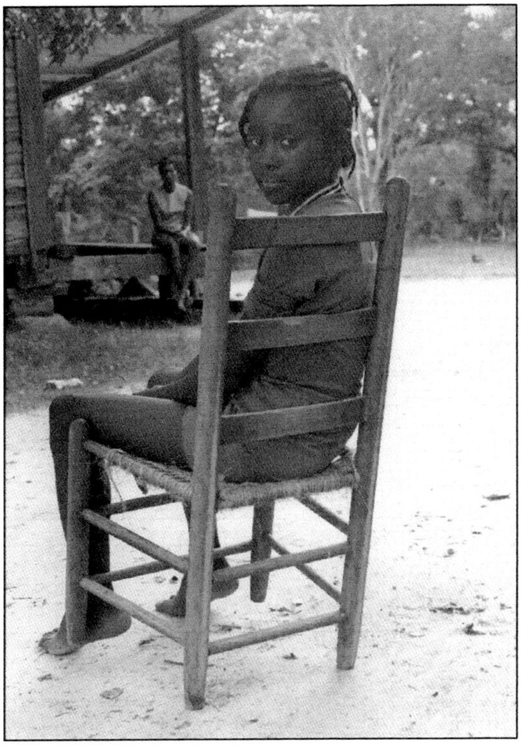

The Depression was hard on everyone and children were no exception.

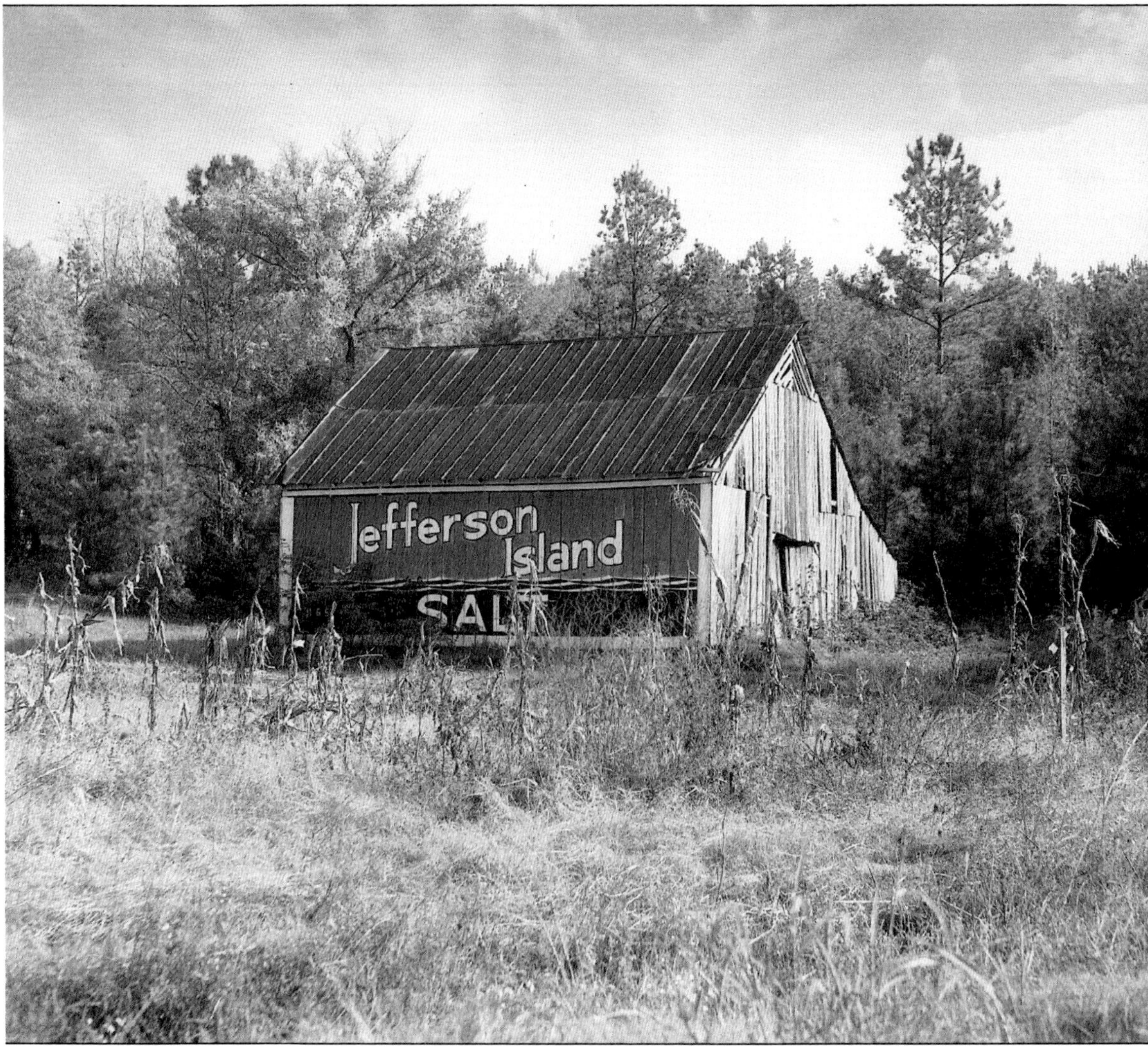

During the Depression in rural America, barns were used for both storage and endorsement.

change, for they had already known hard times for almost a decade.

Linked with the Depression are sharecropping and tenant farming. Neither system was self-perpetuating, but fed upon itself and, in the process, drained both the land and its inhabitants. Both systems presented a terrible problem because no longer could a good living be made with a mule and 40 acres. A common lament of the farmer was:

Eleven cent cotton, forty cent meat
How in the Hell can a poor man eat
Pray for sunshine, course it's gonna rain.
Things gittin worse—driven all insane;
Built a nice barn, painted it brown;
Lightning came along and burnt it down
No use talkin! Any man's beat
With 'leven cent cotton and forty cent meat.[4]

Even with the uncertain conditions of farming, it still provided a better opportunity than no job at all. Though farming was a hard life, it enabled poor whites and blacks to eke out a living.

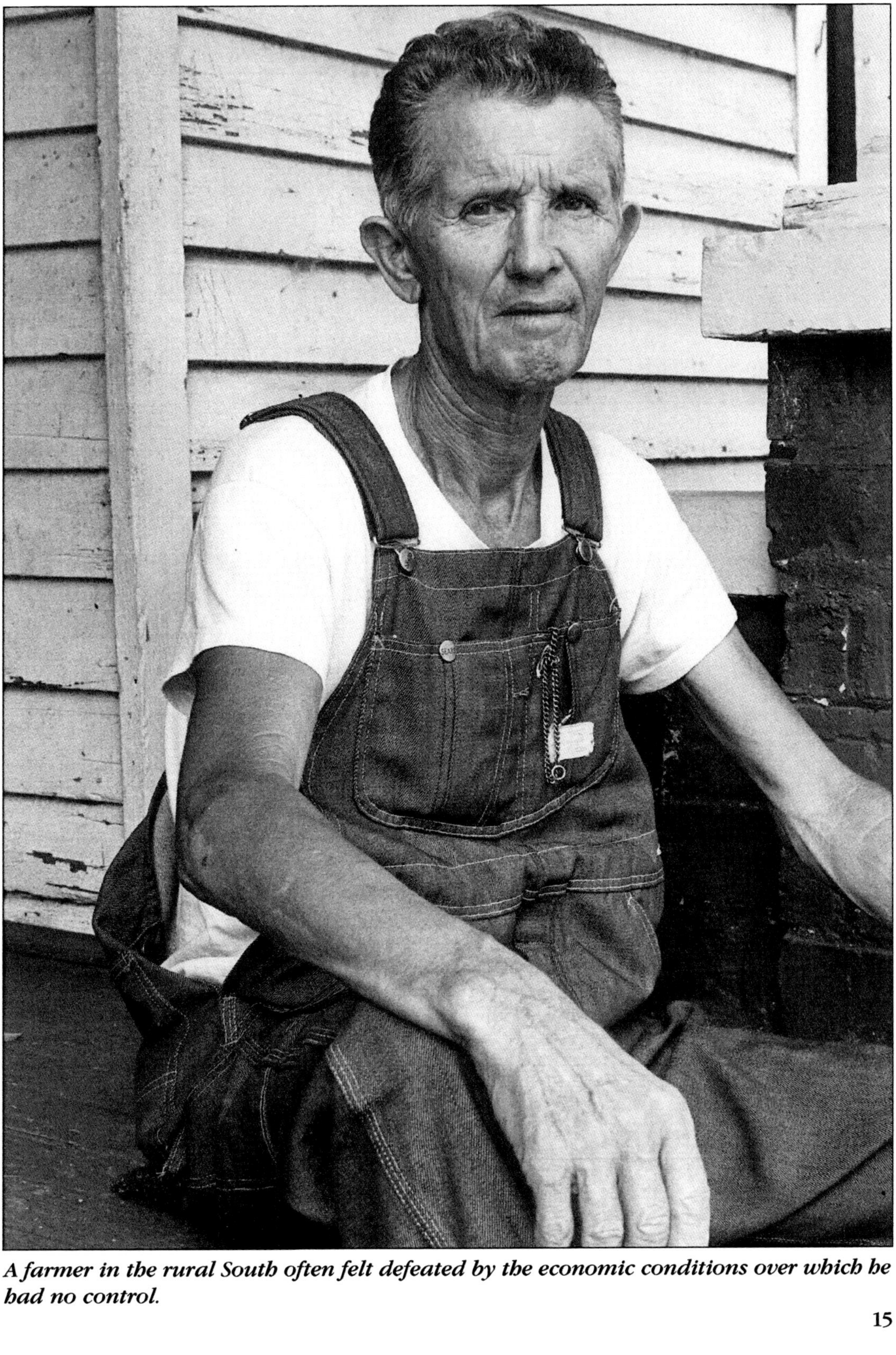

A farmer in the rural South often felt defeated by the economic conditions over which he had no control.

When the Depression overtook the nation in 1929, it brought a questioning of the American way of life; a questioning deeper than at any other time since the Civil War. Perhaps too deep for the average citizen to understand, the floods of disaster had rolled across the landscape and erased the tidemarks of inherited wisdom from the past.

The world of the 1930s was a strange, new world. Following in the footsteps of the flamboyant Roaring Twenties, characterized by the "flappers" and the "jazz age," the lean, niggardly world of the 1930s was even more of an astonishment.

Through constant tribulation, everything in the life of the common man during this period produced frustration. He felt defeated. He felt the despair and dejection that came from defeat. Out of his predicament grew desperation, and out of desperation grew resentment. His bitterness was a taste his tongue would always have.

The world would never again be the old, fixed, certain, familiar and lazy world that was known before 1914. Strange new ideas were sweeping through the land, and all the old faiths and beliefs were under attack, crumbling, or even vanishing in places. Doubt, change, and violence were everywhere. (5)

Stereotypes of thought, traditional life, and the collected wisdom of the elders all were challenged in books, magazines, and private talk. Perhaps, after all, the promise of American life would turn out really to be propaganda, the tyranny of words or the folklore of capitalism.

A generation growing up in these conditions could not help but be changed by such foreboding circumstances. It was a period in which new trends of thought emerged in economic matters, social activity and moral conduct—all leaving the pockmark of progress upon the nation's young.

But while youth was prone to rebel, middle-age individuals often clung all the more firmly to old loyalties, leaping to the defense of hard work, thrift, and individual enterprise; and opposing change in these concepts of law and government, which they associated with happier days.

During the Great Depression, such conditions of poverty were ever-prevailing. Poverty (both mental, emotional, and financial) had wrought its effect upon a nation of people—people who would never forget their frustrations, apathy, and resentment during the terrible years of the Great Depression.

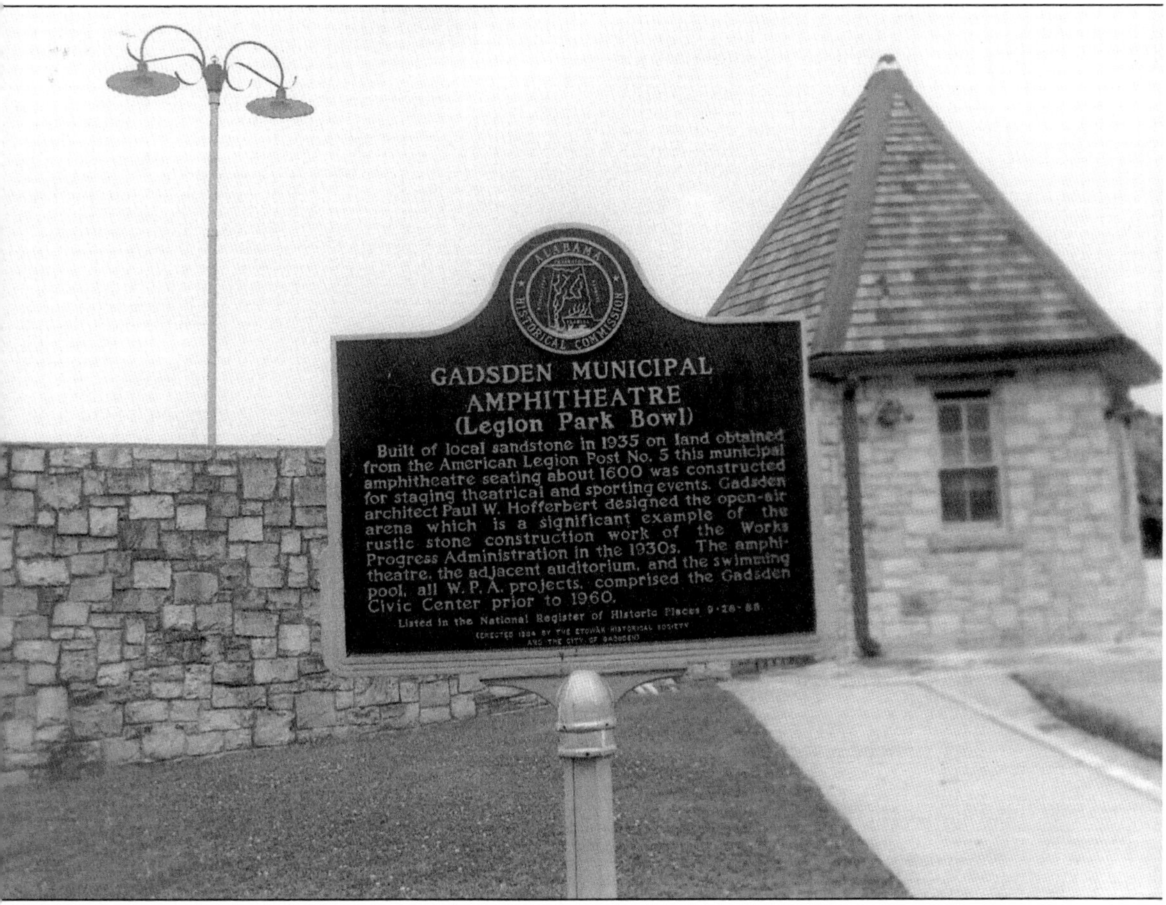

The Gadsden Municipal Amphitheater was built of local sandstone in 1935 by the WPA.

WPA

After the stock market crash of 1929, the Depression was on and conditions continued to worsen each year. The years of 1932 and 1933 were the worst, with high unemployment nationwide.

An already bad situation was magnified when banks began foreclosing on overdue loans, causing the loss of homes, farms, and businesses. To complicate matters, people across the country were making a run on the banks, withdrawing their money suddenly. This caused many to run out of cash and close for ever.

In 1932 Franklin D. Roosevelt was elected president. After assuming office the next year, one of his first acts as president was to declare a bank holiday, which closed all financial institutions until the drastic conditions could be rectified.

After this start, the president then moved on to what he labeled the New Deal. This was a series of social programs designed to ease the heavy burden the people of this nation were experiencing.

One of the first programs Roosevelt created was the WPA. It was designed to provide work for the unemployed and, at the same time, to improve communities across the country.

While much of the work done by the WPA was temporary and is no longer visible,

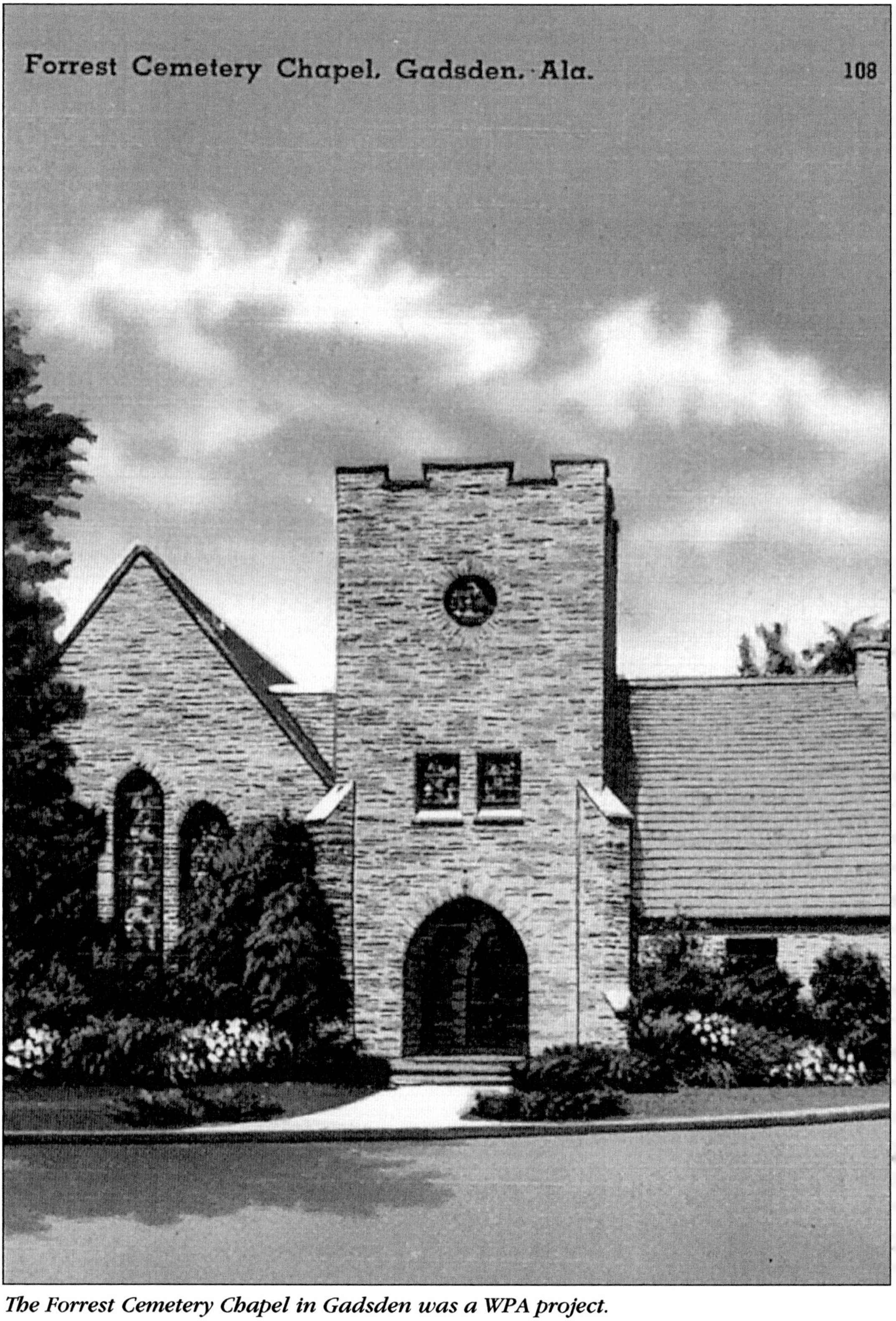

The Forrest Cemetery Chapel in Gadsden was a WPA project.

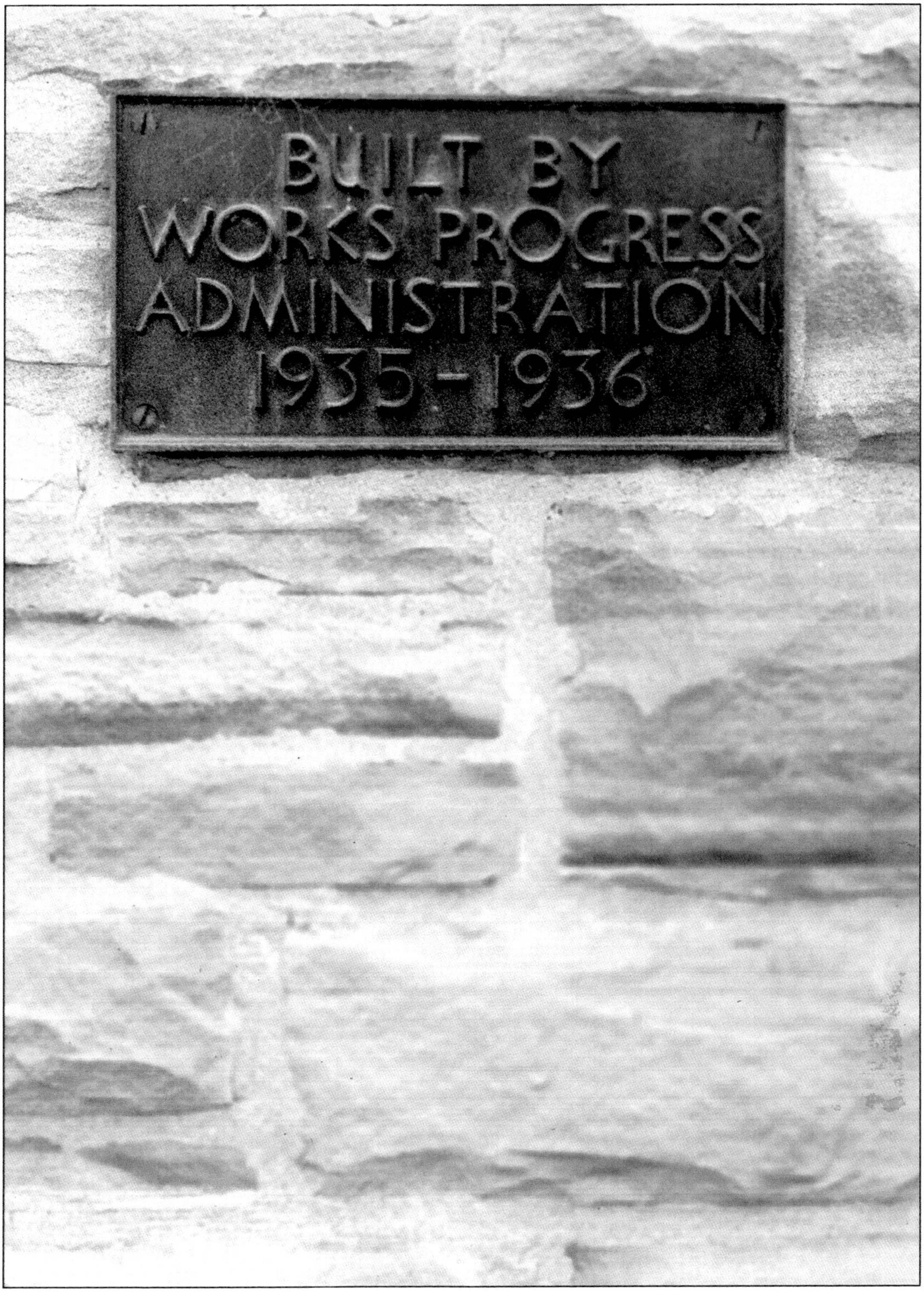

This marker serves as a permanent record of a WPA project at the Forrest Cemetery Chapel.

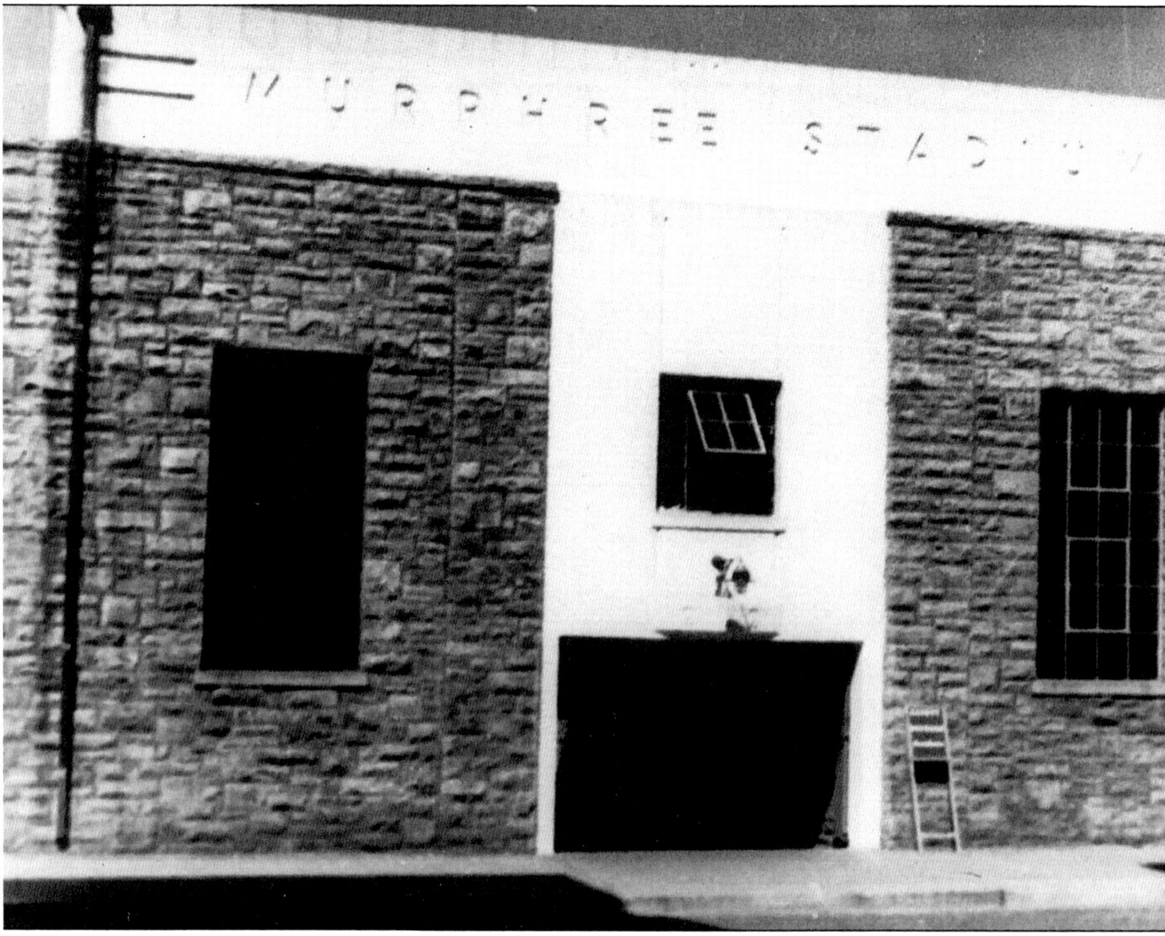

Murphrae Stadium, behind Gadsden High School, was constructed by WPA labor from local sandstone in the 1930s.

such as cleaning out drainage ditches or improving the roads, there was another, more permanent phase in which the WPA was responsible for the construction of buildings. Since there was an abundance of sandstone in some areas, many of these WPA-made structures were produced from this available material.

The Depression was tough. Although the WPA didn't solve all the problems of that era, it did provide a meager income for many families, restored a measure of dignity to those who were employed, and provided physical improvements that are still evident today.

When the offspring of the Depression view these buildings, they are reminded of a time in American history when the government and the people worked together.

During a period of extreme hardship, a period of suffering for all, each personal sacrifice strengthened the national character and, in the process, built a better society for everyone in the generations to follow.

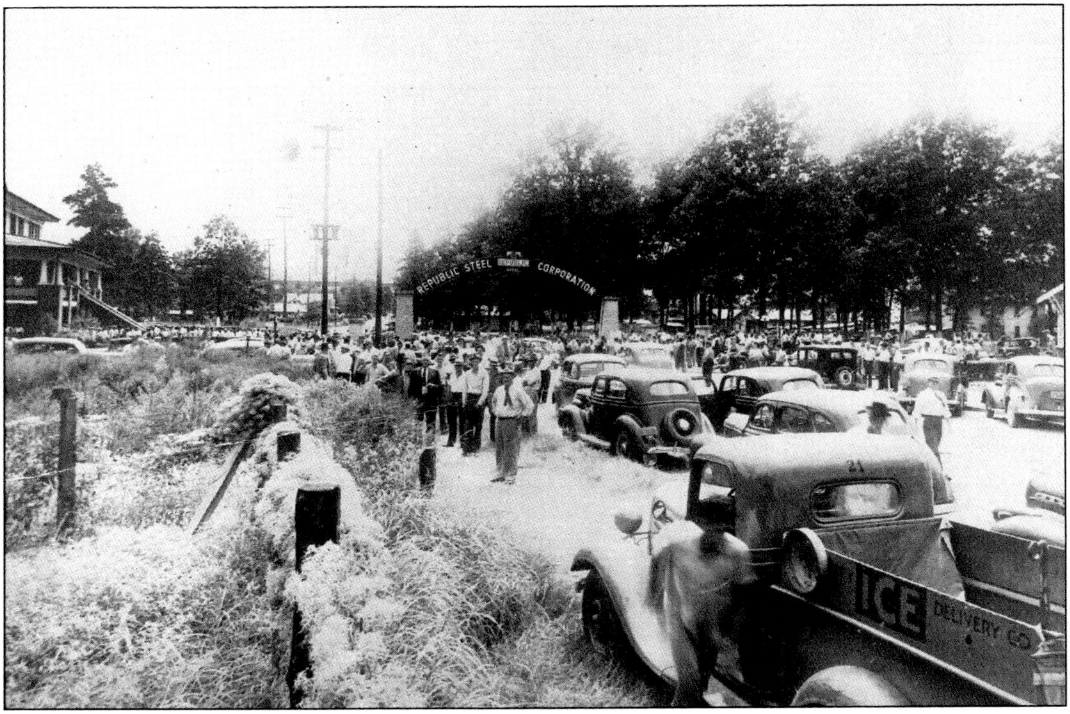

This strike occurred at the Republic Steel Corporation.

UNIONS

The 1930s brought about a revolution in the labor movement. Until that time, labor was represented by the American Federation of Labor and was organized by specific crafts. These included skilled workers like brickmasons, carpenters, barbers, electricians, and machinists.

In 1935, Congress passed the National Labor Relations Act, known also as the Wagner Act, and President Roosevelt signed it into law. This law was designed to protect the rights of unions.

About this same time, a split developed in the AFL over how to organize the large manufacturing plants; whether by crafts or by industries. Due to this problem, a number of leaders broke away from the AFL and formed the CIO. This group set out to organize the bigger industries such as automobile, steel, coal mining, and rubber.

By law, the unions had every right to organize; however, companies did everything they possibly could to prevent this, with management trying to keep the workers from organizing. In some cases, this conflict would turn violent and, like the Civil War, many times it would pit brother against brother, or father against son.

In this heated environment, sometimes there would be a walkout by the workers and picket lines thrown up. When management personnel or sympathetic company workers would try to cross the picket line, it often resulted in violence. The police would be called in to settle the dispute and, if successful, business could proceed.

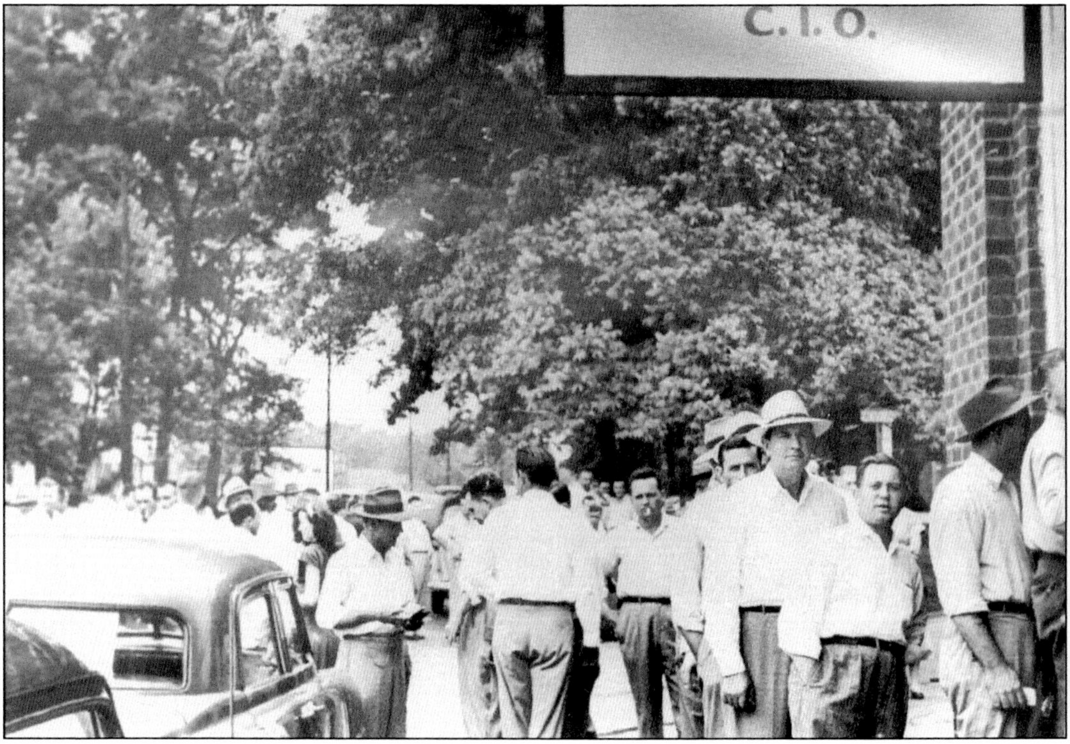

The CIO was an organization for big industries, such as automobile, steel, and rubber.

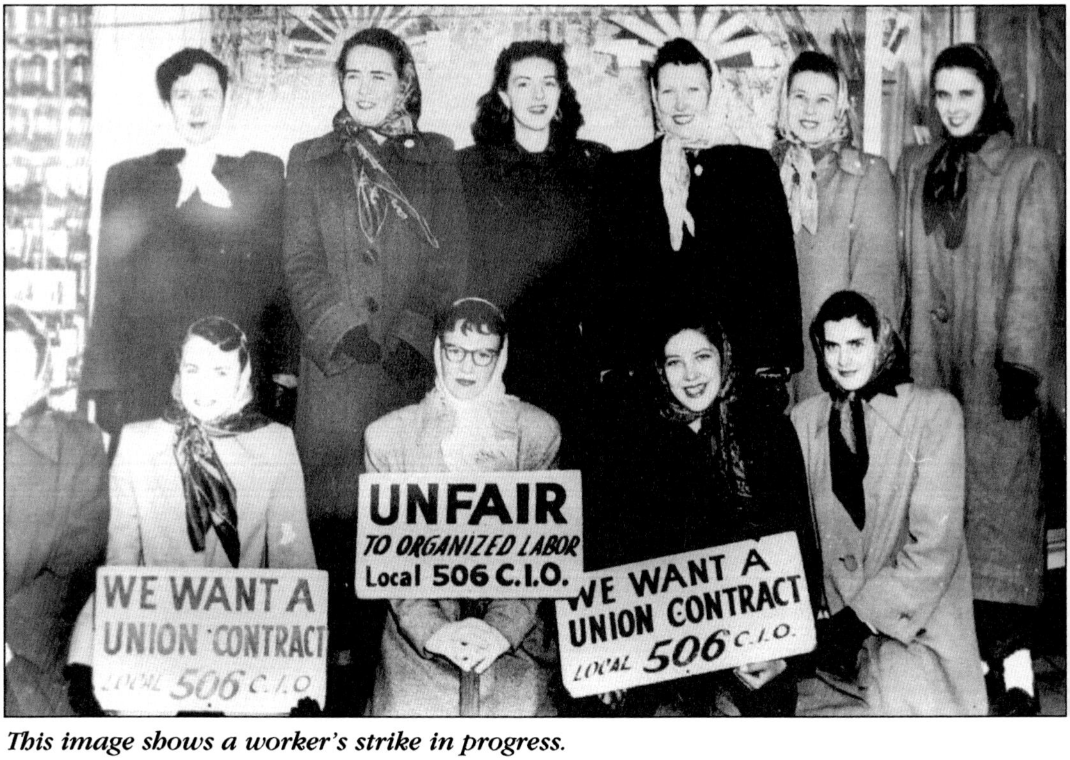

This image shows a worker's strike in progress.

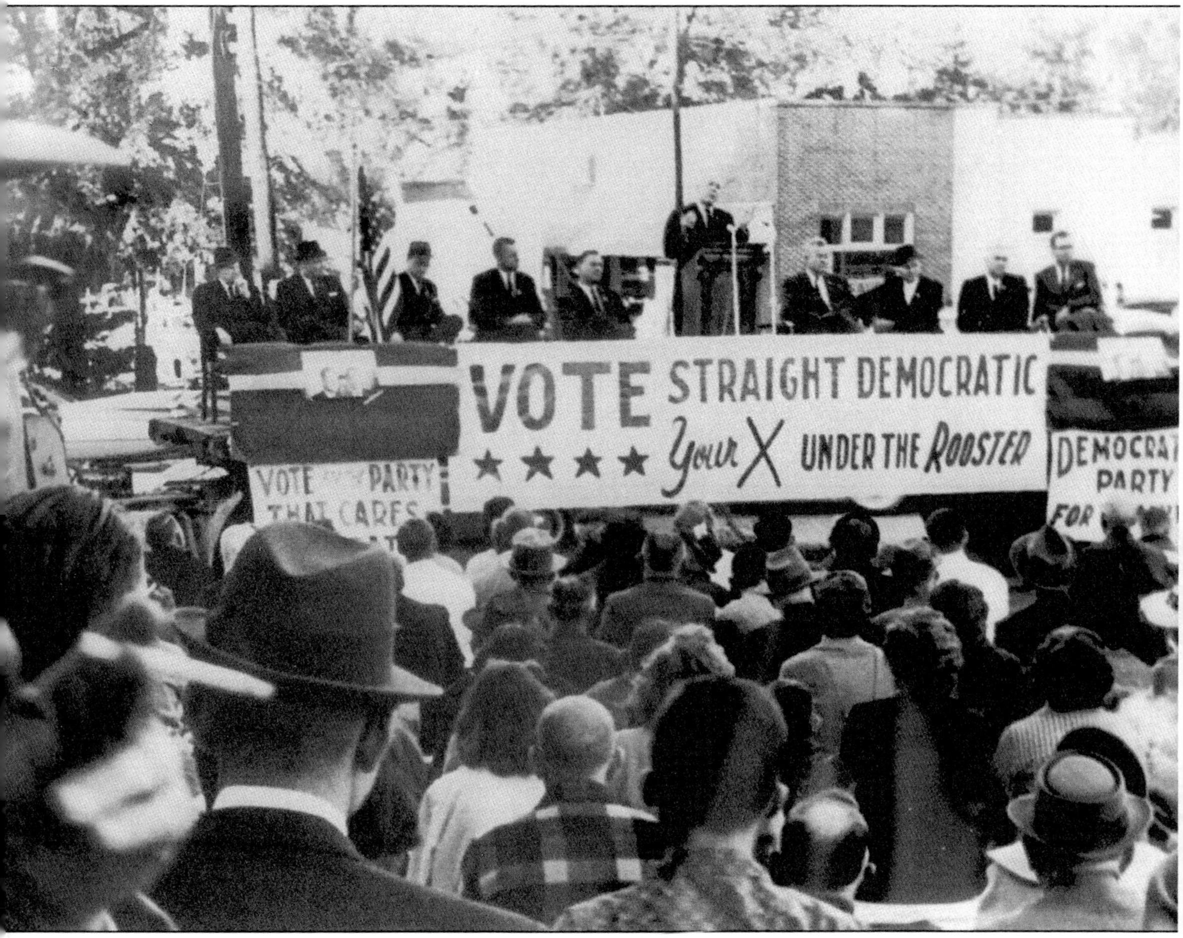

This political rally was trying to promote voting "under the rooster."

Politics

Starting with the end of the Civil War, Southern politicians became steadfast Democrats; this was never truer than during the Depression. With Franklin D. Roosevelt leading from the White House, the national scene also favored the Democratic Party and this trend filtered down to the local level.

During this era, many people in the country were unable to read; so to instruct their voters on how to cast a ballot, the Democratic Party used a symbol—a rooster. All the Democratic campaign advertising stressed voting "under the rooster," and at the top of the ballot for Democratic candidates would be a picture of a rooster.

At election time, a Democratic primary was held and if no one received a majority of votes, a runoff was held between the two top candidates. Since there was only this one primary, there was really no philosophical difference between the candidates; the race simply became a personality contest.

In this county, during one election, the race for tax assessor produced a tie vote. To break the standoff, the winner was ultimately decided by the toss of a coin. Ironically, four years later these same two men ran again for this office and the man who lost the first race by a coin toss won the second time around.

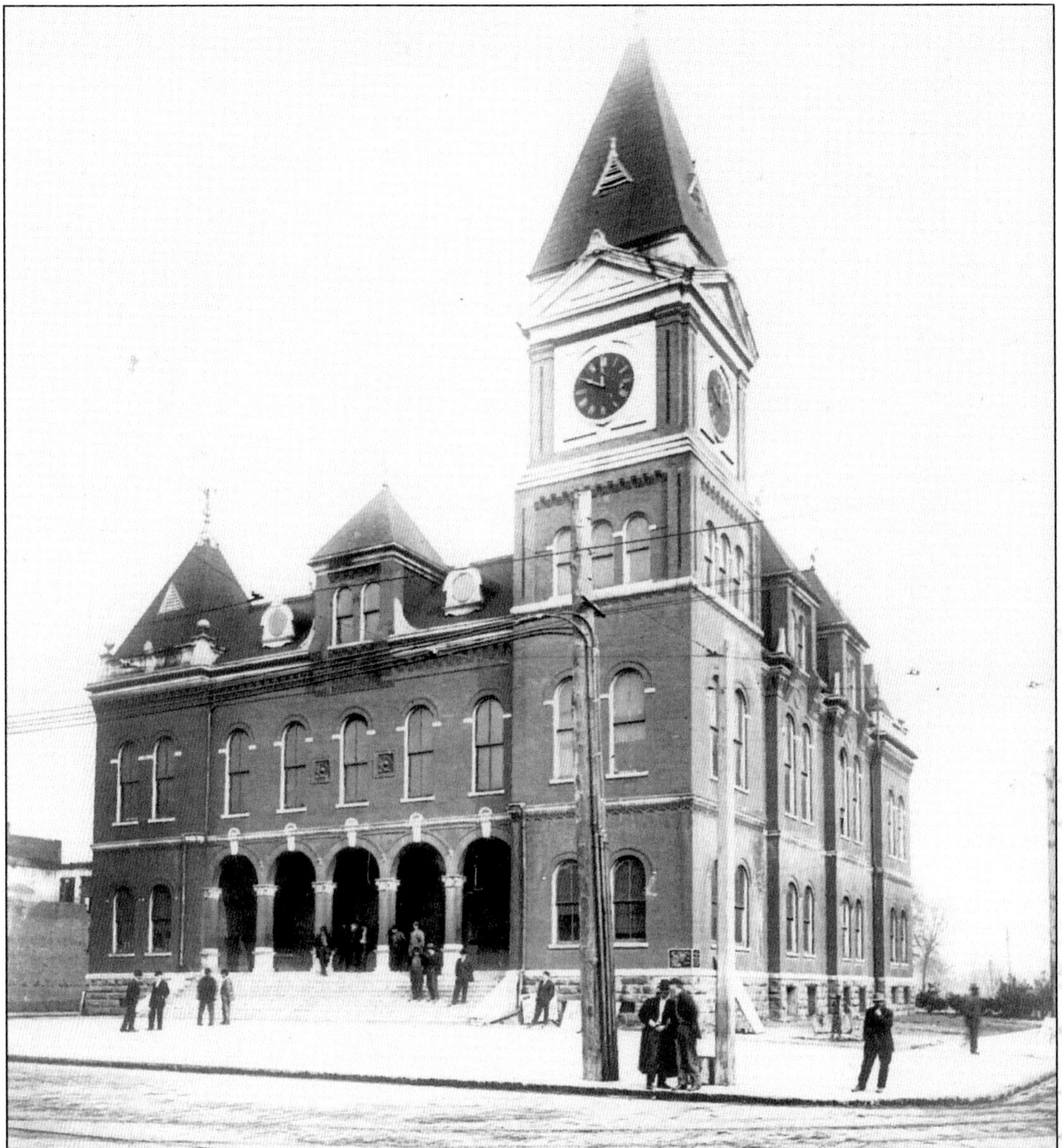

The old Etowah County courthouse in Gadsden was the seat of local government. In those days, political candidates frequently spoke from the steps.

With no opposition, the victor from the Democratic primary was always the winner since there was no Republican candidate, except in the case of a presidential race.

In the days before media consultants and professional handlers advised the politicians on how to conduct themselves before the public, campaigns produced some interesting and heated races; although usually between members of the same political party.

Today, political primaries are still tough battlegrounds, but it is much better to actually have a choice between two different governing philosophies than just between two different personalities, or to be instructed to cast your vote "under the rooster."

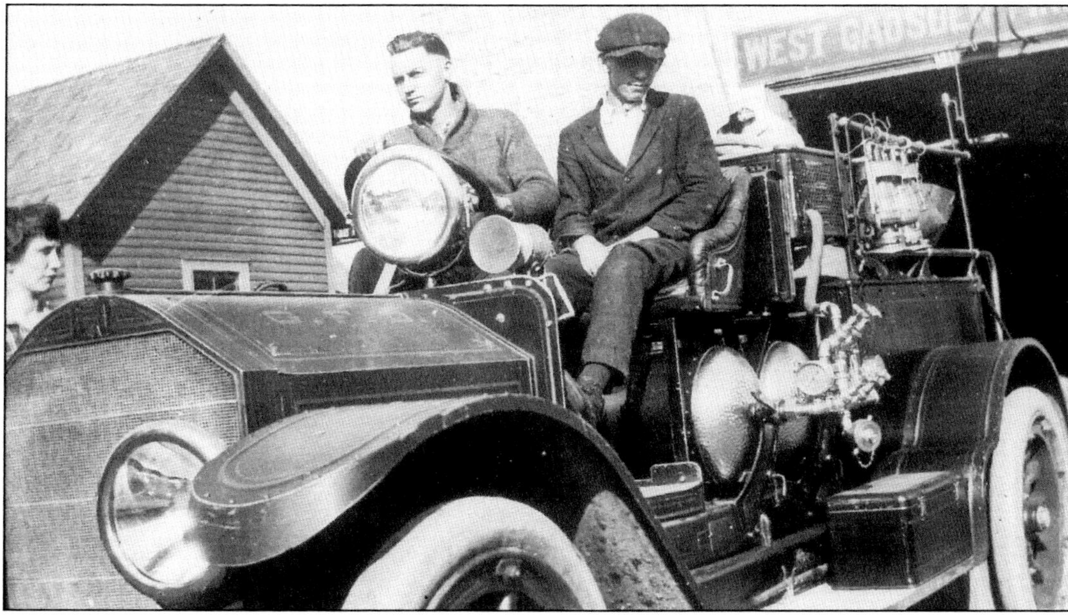

Some of the "professors" from the "institution of higher learning," the West Gadsden Fire Hall, appear on this fire engine.

INSTITUTION OF HIGHER LEARNING

A lot of men were unemployed during the Depression and, with time on their hands, needed a place to go each day. While almost any location would suffice—a gas station, a street corner, a country store, or a library—one of the most popular destinations was the fire hall.

For the people who spent their days around the fire hall, it became more than just a social center. For the children, especially, it was an educational experience.

"My family lived five houses from the fire hall," my father said, "and it was a hangout for both men and boys. I considered it a great institution of higher learning because of the varied discussions we had, since these were topics you never read about in books."

The Depression era was a time when large numbers of men smoked. A Target cigarette rolling machine was kept at the fire hall, so this was a natural "draw" for many men who bought Target tobacco (which came with rolling papers) and could roll themselves a supply of cigarettes.

Those who couldn't afford the luxury of Target, would hand-roll their own cigarettes from Bull Durham or Golden Grain. Both of these tobaccos came in a small cotton bag with a drawstring and rolling papers.

To hand-roll a cigarette took some coordination. Since it occupied both hands, after spreading the tobacco onto the rolling paper the man would put the drawstring in his teeth and give it a pull, to close off his bag.

While a checker game was always in progress, the biggest attraction of the fire hall was decent conversation and, many times, arguments.

A favorite fire hall topic was sports. In the fall, it was football, especially concerning Alabama since their team went to the Rose Bowl twice in the 1930s. During spring and summer, baseball talk dominated, and was mostly about the Saint Louis "Cardinals" and the Philadelphia "Athletics."

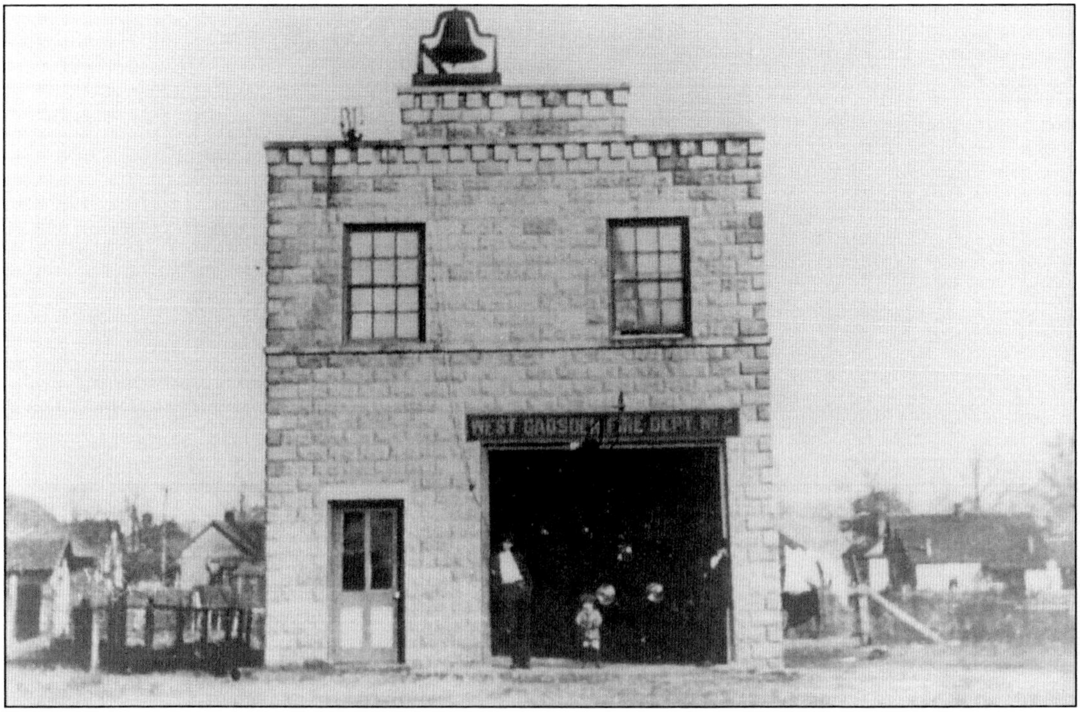

The West Gadsden Fire Hall became an "institution of higher learning" for many young boys during the Depression.

As players, the "Cardinals" had "Dizzy" Paul Dean, "Pepper" Martin, and "Wild Bill" Halihan, while the "Athletics" had Mickey Cochran, "Lefty" Grove, and George Ernshaw.

As imagined, another favorite topic of conversation for men around the fire hall was hunting and fishing.

"Although I received much education pertaining to sports, fox hunting and fishing, the real education was from the 'great debates'," my father reported.

"These would be 'deep' subjects such as: If a squirrel is in a tree and a hunter on the ground, while they both keep moving around the same tree, does the hunter ever go around the squirrel?"

A similar argument concerned a fly in a moving train coach, and how fast the fly was traveling if the coach was sitting still, in motion, or if the fly was heading in the opposite direction?

There were discussions in the fire hall about whether the earth was round or flat. The flat-earth crew testified that if it were round, everybody would fall off. They bolstered their case with the Biblical reference to "the four corners of the earth."

As counterpoint, the other side held the opinion of a round earth because, if a person started at one point and continued in that direction, eventually they would return to the point of origin.

At the fire hall, this type of "reasoning" would go on for hours; but since these men didn't have anything else to occupy their time, which side really won or lost was not the point.

Because these men were just killing time, no one knew if they really believed what they were arguing or simply taking a position to keep the discussion going.

"I really feel sorry for all those unfortunate people who didn't experience the tremendous education that was available in this institution of higher learning—the fire hall," my father stated.

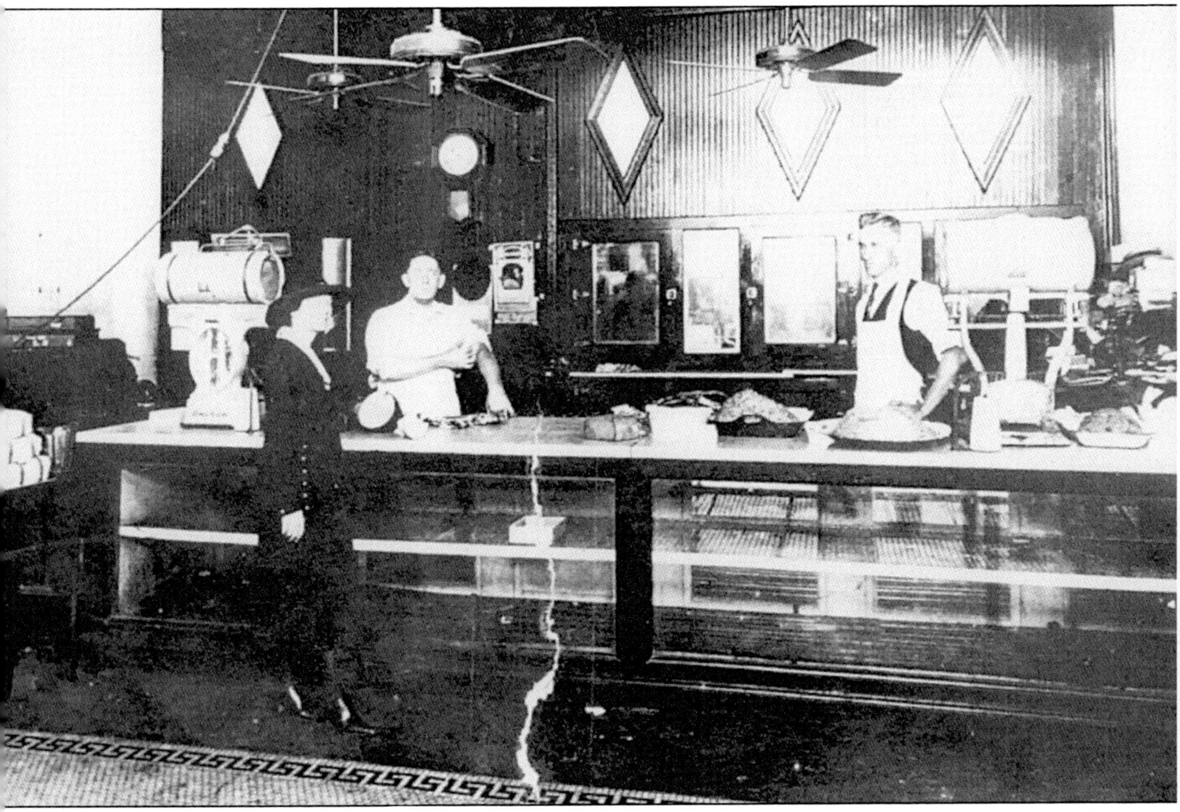

The butchers at a meat market were extremely accurate when it came to judging amounts for their customers.

Grocery Store

In the early years of this century, with its small towns and neighborhoods, it was the grocery store that brought together a community. During my father's youth, all the grocery stores were "Mom-and-Pop" operations.

While there might be many stores, each one was a small, separate business operating independently from the others. In his old neighborhood, there were at least five of these "Mom-and-Pop" operations within two blocks of his home.

In those days, most of the grocery stores had a front porch. On the porch some products were displayed for sale, such as produce or bundles of kindling, tied with bailing wire.

On the inside of the store, the selection was limited. With the Depression in full swing, operating a small grocery store was difficult. Sometimes there was almost no choice, with only one brand of a particular product available. At other times there would be more to buy, but the customers would have no money for a purchase.

When they did, the most basic items sold were sugar, salt, coffee, and flour, while the youngsters favored candy jawbreakers, orange slices, peppermint sticks and peanut brittle.

The customers at a small grocery store did not have to select their own groceries. Instead, they would tell the clerk what they wanted and he would gather it up for them to take home in a paper sack.

Before the days of mass marketing, many of the items were not prepackaged, but were for sale in bulk form—items such as

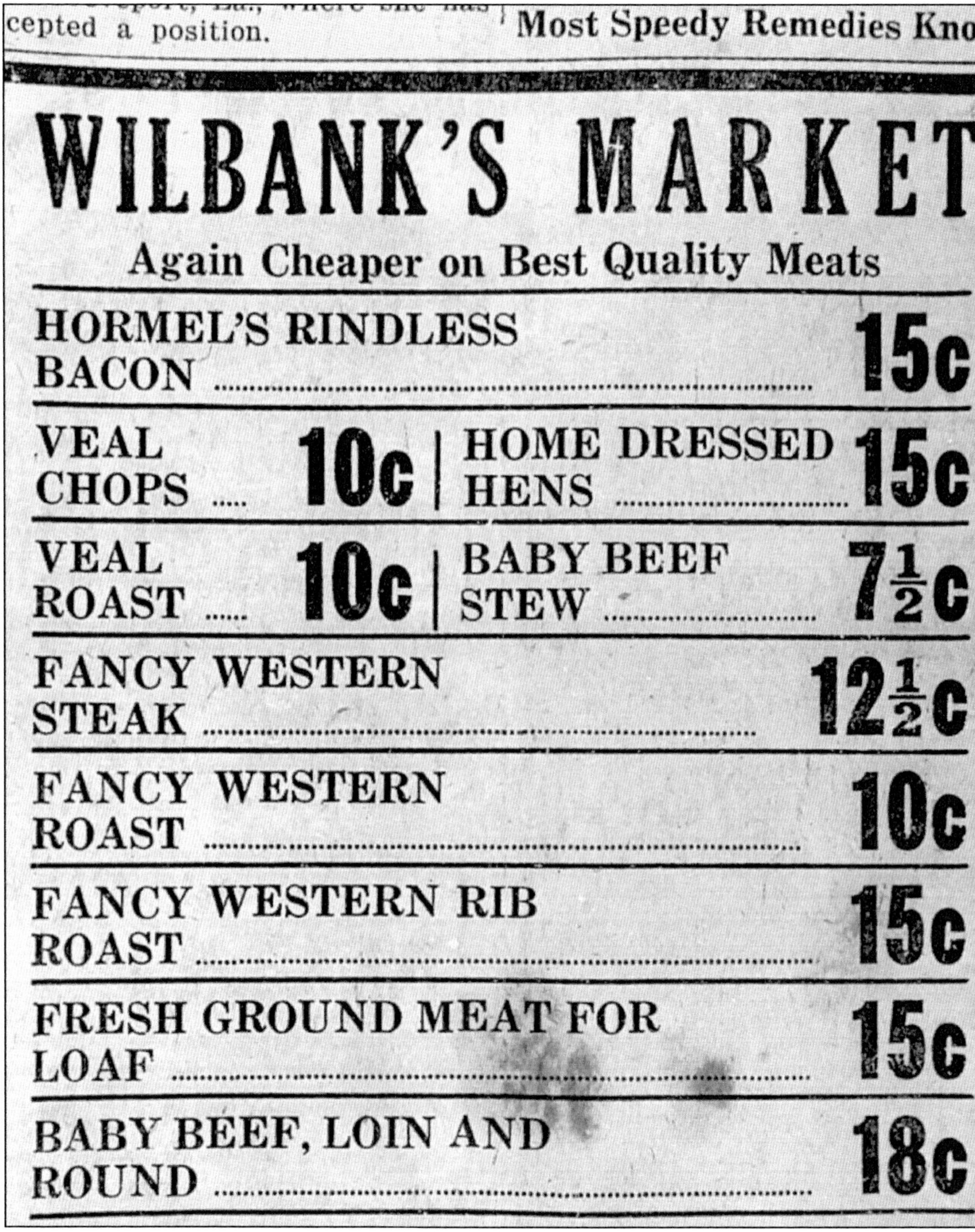

cepted a position. | Most Speedy Remedies Kno

WILBANK'S MARKET

Again Cheaper on Best Quality Meats

HORMEL'S RINDLESS BACON 15c

VEAL CHOPS ..... 10c | HOME DRESSED HENS 15c

VEAL ROAST ..... 10c | BABY BEEF STEW 7½c

FANCY WESTERN STEAK 12½c

FANCY WESTERN ROAST 10c

FANCY WESTERN RIB ROAST 15c

FRESH GROUND MEAT FOR LOAF 15c

BABY BEEF, LOIN AND ROUND 18c

During the 1930s, Wilbank's Meat Market was located on lower Broad Street in Gadsden.

dried beans and sugar. Whatever specific amount was needed it would be weighed, put into a paper sack, and tied off with string; the string pulled down from a large ball that was suspended from the ceiling.

For the youngsters, one of the most memorable parts of the store was the candy counter. It consisted of a glass display case, so all the candy could be seen; from this selection the children would choose whatever goodies caught their eye.

Most of the candy in the case was "penny candy," so-called because each piece sold for one cent. To stand before that candy case, with a nickel in hand and try to decide what to buy, was always a tough decision.

Another attraction of the candy counter was "prize candy." This special candy was round and flat (like a peppermint today), with a chocolate covering and a white or pink filling.

The child would choose which piece he wanted and break it open. If it had a white center he didn't win anything, but if it had a pink center, he was a winner! Normally, the prize was some type of candy bar.

There was also a second prize that was given to the person who bought the last piece of candy, and that was usually a smaller candy bar than the first prize.

Since money was in short supply, all groceries were bought on credit and settled up each payday. When the bill was paid, most store owners would go to the candy case and select a few pieces of candy, as a reward for the family's children.

Back then, an interesting service offered by some neighborhood stores was to send a clerk by specific homes each morning to take an order for groceries. After they would make the rounds of all their customers, the clerk would return to the store, gather up these orders, and deliver them in the afternoon.

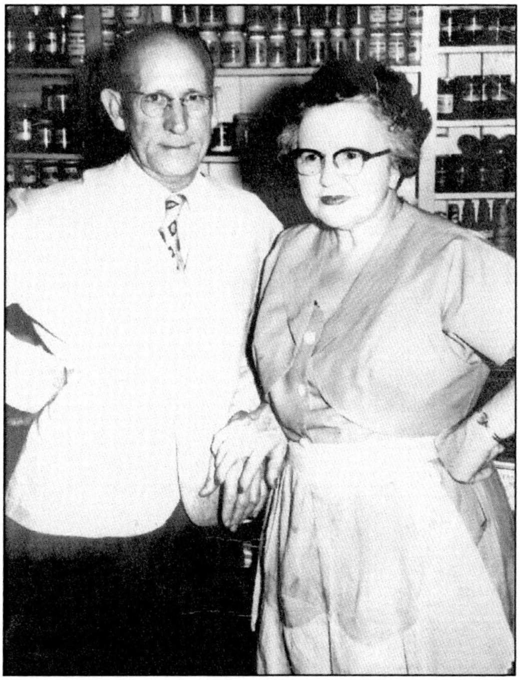

Woody and Bessie Duncan operated a "Mom-and-Pop" grocery store in the same West Gadsden neighborhood for over 40 years.

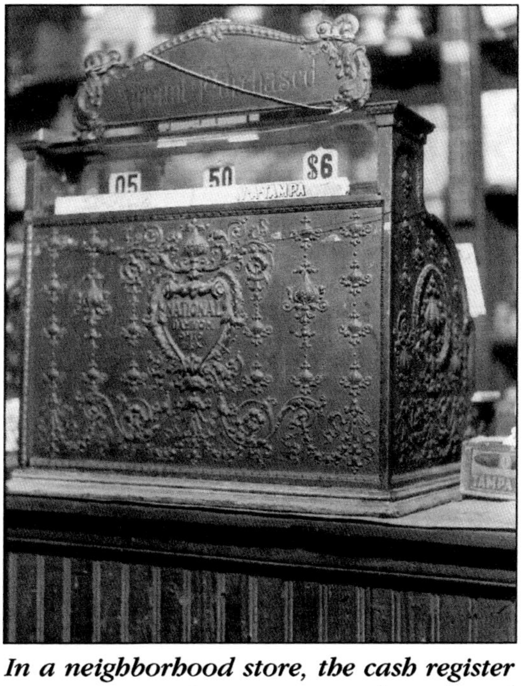

In a neighborhood store, the cash register was a prized possession that lasted for generations.

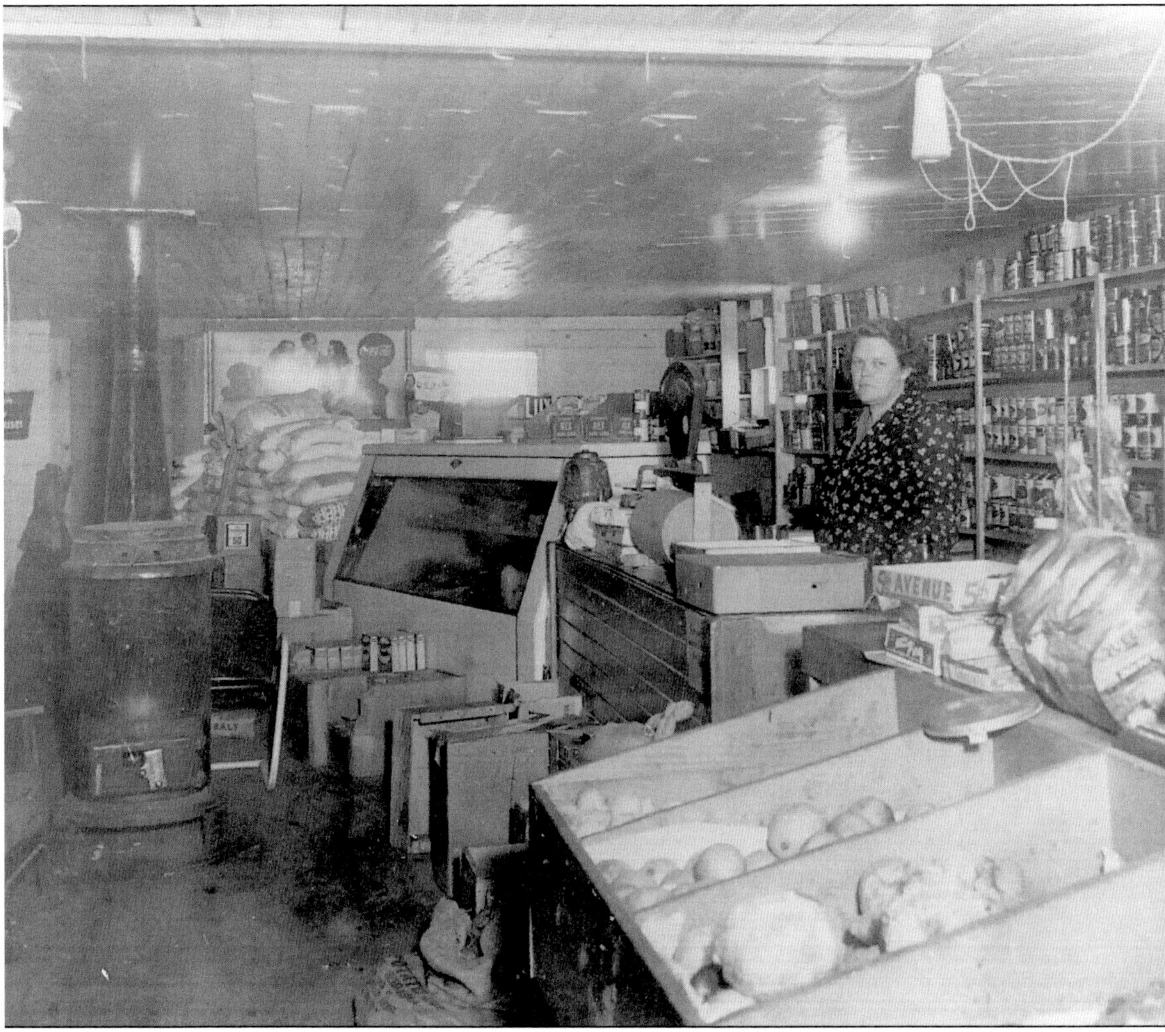

The inside of a neighborhood grocery store was a world unto itself.

While there might be many grocery stores in a neighborhood, not all of them included a meat market. However, for those that did, the meats were kept in a cooler. If a customer wanted a roast or a steak, the owner would bring out a quarter of beef, place it on the butcher block, and cut whatever amount was requested.

It was amazing how accurate these butchers were. If the patron wanted a three-pound roast, with his skilled eye, the butcher would probably not miss it by more than one or two ounces!

The grocery store was always a great place to meet your neighbors and exchange the daily news, because the grocer could pass along events of the neighborhood; such as who was sick or out of town visiting relatives.

Likewise, the grocer was more than just a store owner; he was often a friend. Possibly, he was a neighbor living down the street and even attended the same church as his customers.

One of the hidden assets of these little stores was how they became such a vital part of the neighborhood. In this friendly environment, each customer knew the grocer and all his other customers; and he knew them and their family from years of

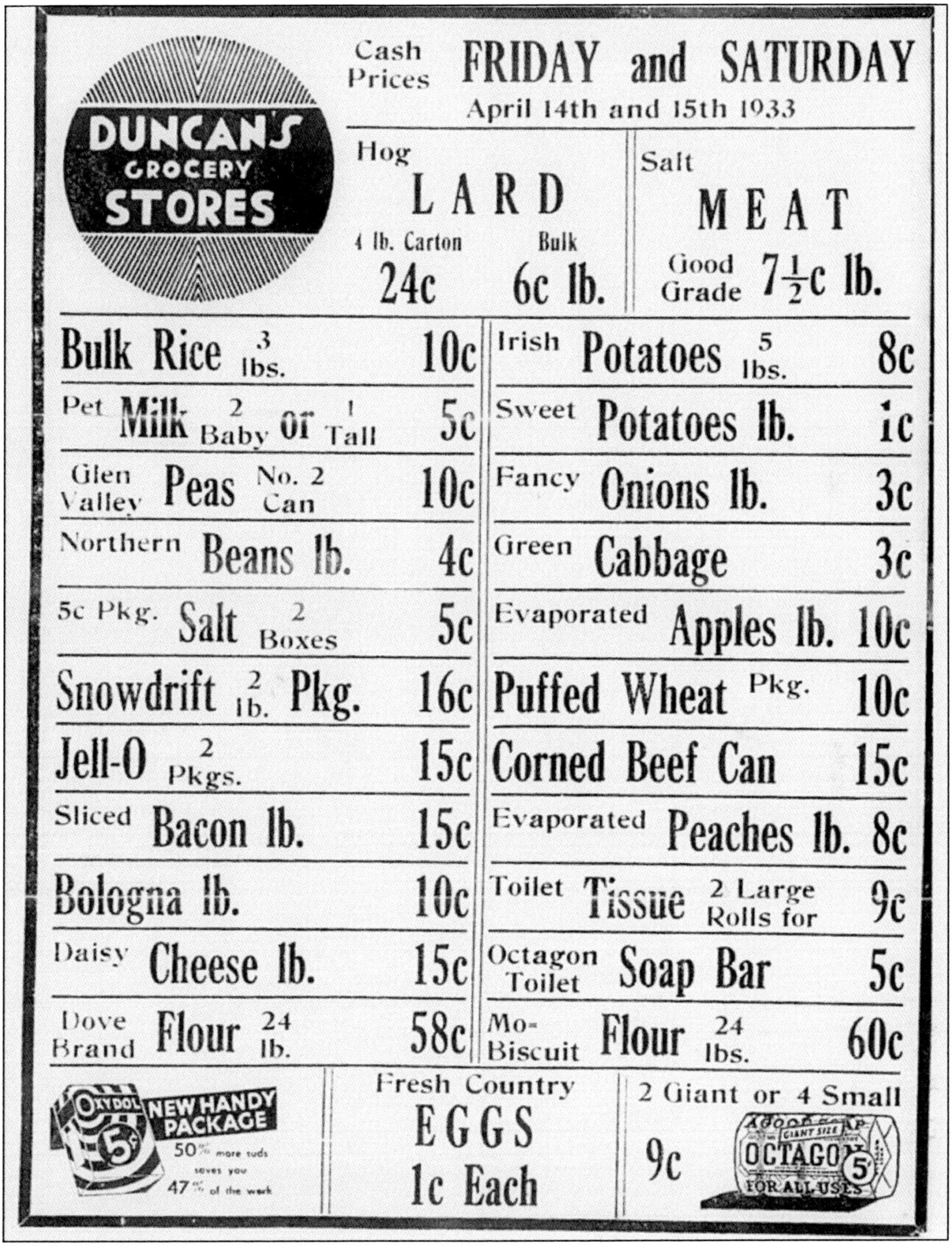

This advertisement came from Duncan's Grocery, c. 1933.

steady association.

With the ever-changing pace of today's world, many sights known to America's past are rapidly disappearing. Such is the fate of the old-fashioned "Mom-and-Pop" grocery store.

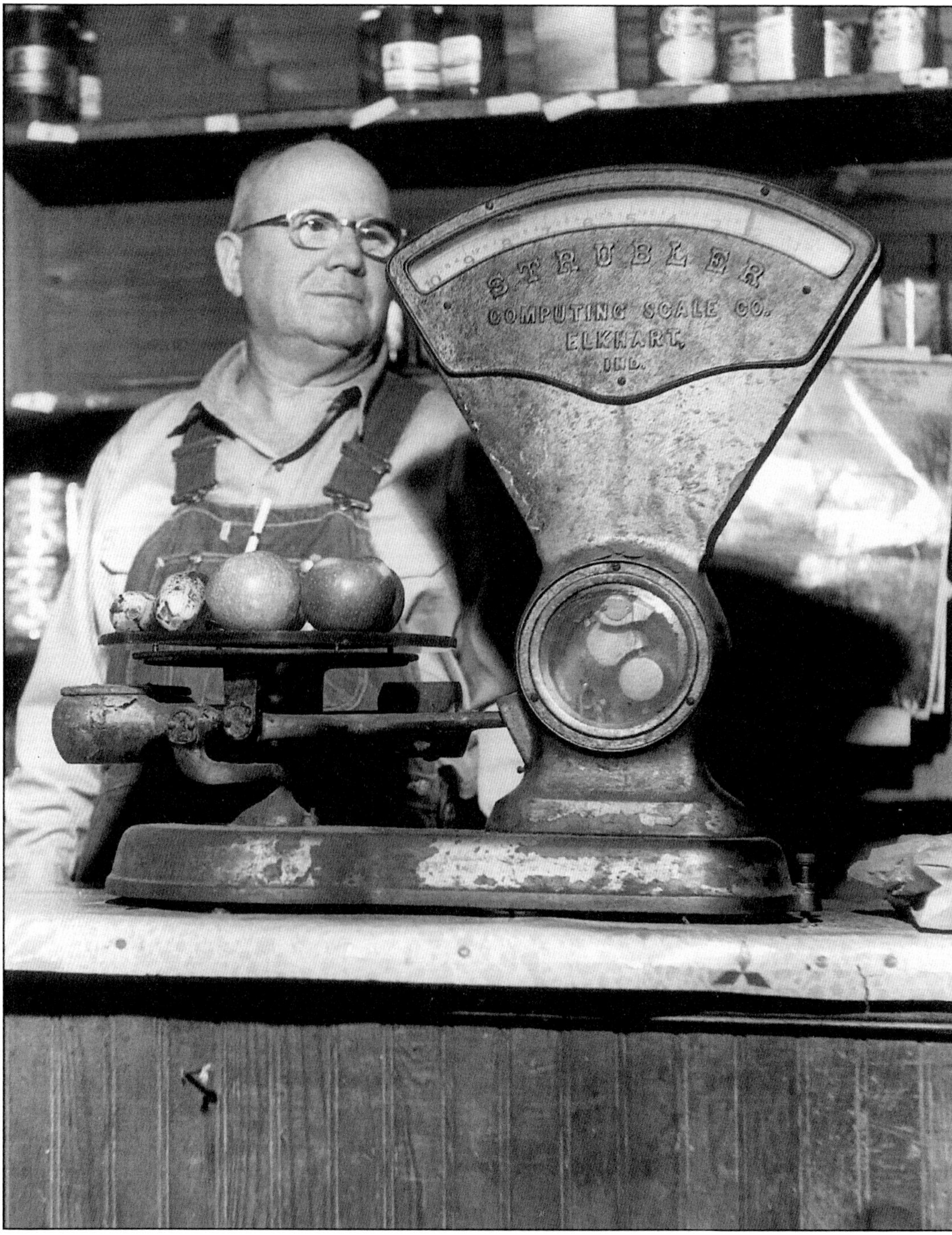

Apples are weighed on an old-fashioned scale by Allen "Buck" Jones.

These small businesses added a distinctive personality to our American past. While they are now a part of history, one can picture a quiet afternoon with the men loafing around the front of the store, and a lazy dog dusting itself in the middle of the road.

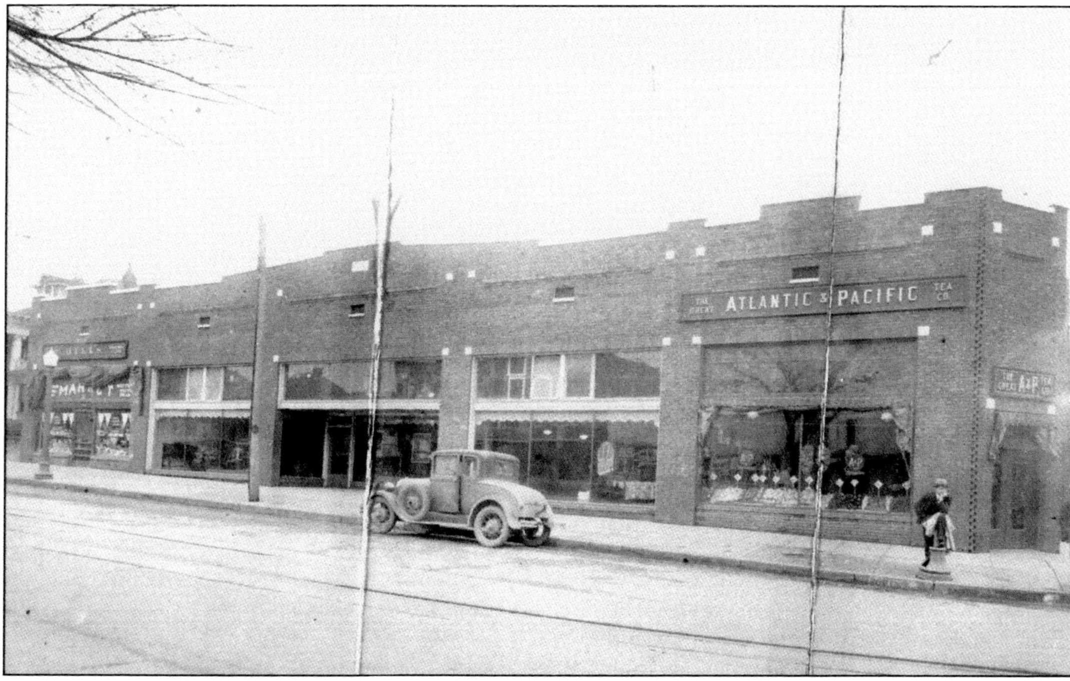

Isbell-Hallmark Furniture is the only store from the "mini-business district" still in operation. In the 1930s, it was flanked by Hill's and A&P Grocery Stores.

MINI-BUSINESS DISTRICT

Throughout the city there were several small areas which consisted of businesses other than "Mom-and-Pop" grocery stores. One of these mini-business districts was located one mile from town and three blocks from my father's house.

In this district were four grocery stores, one meat market, a service station, a beauty shop, two dry cleaners, two furniture stores, two barber shops, a drug store, and an ice plant.

Connected to the ice plant was an ice cream parlor, which served Eskimo Pies as well as ice cream bars; and, during the season, ice-cold watermelons.

A popular feature provided by the drug store was curb service. A customer would drive up in front of the store, toot the horn and a curb boy would come to take the order. This job was called "hoppin' curb."

Since the drug store had a soda fountain, the curb boy would fill the order at the fountain, then bring it out on a tray, which hooked over the car's window.

The drug store was located on the corner and stayed open until nine p.m. This corner became a hangout for the boys in the neighborhood. If a person didn't have anything to do in the evening, he could go to "the corner" and there would always be other boys there, ready to talk and just pass the time of day.

As a place where the boys congregated, guess who else showed up? A lot of nights the girls would drop by "the corner" to check out the friendly scene. Who knows how many budding romances started on this corner, right in the neighborhood?

Similar to the curb service at the drug store, some of the dry cleaners had a boy who "hustled dry cleaning." He would go around on his bicycle to people's homes, picking up clothes that needed cleaning. He would take the dirty clothes and usually return the cleaned ones that same day.

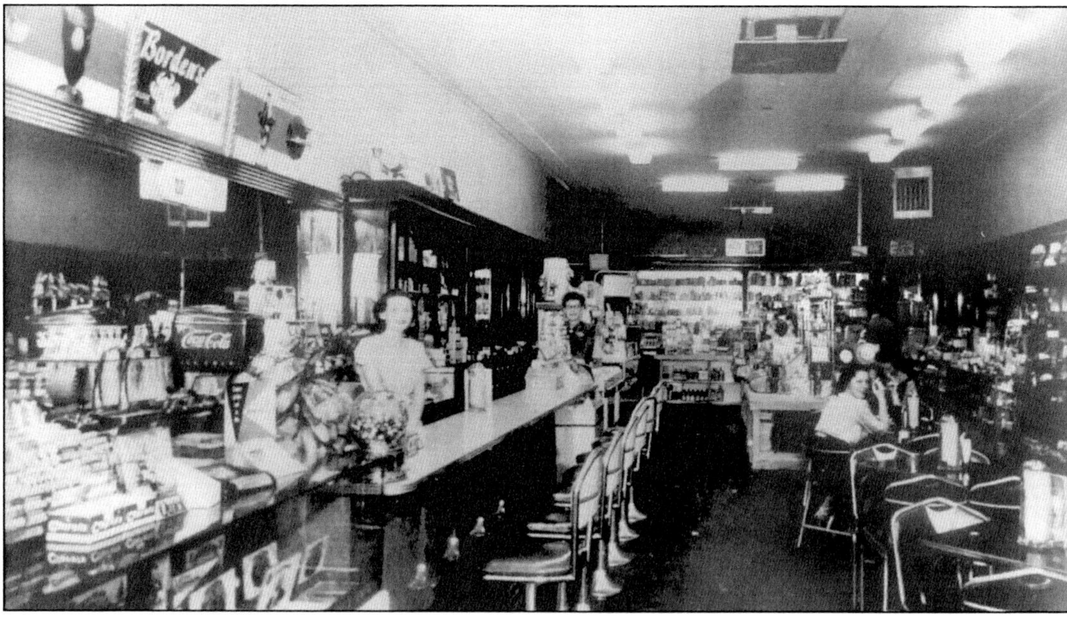

The corner drugstore was a hangout for boys and girls in the neighborhood.

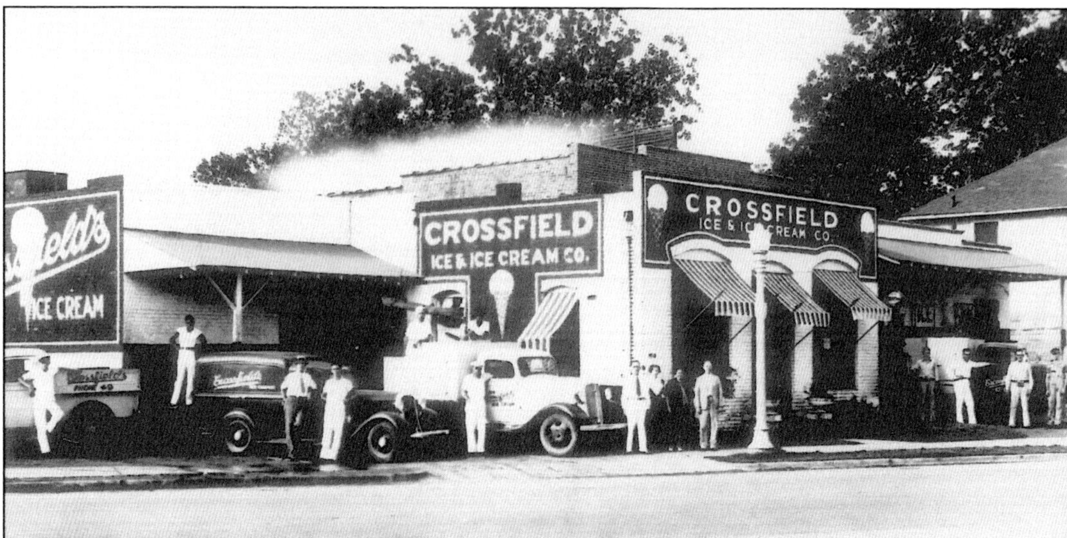

Crossfield Ice Plant had an ice cream parlor connected to it. In season, it also sold cold watermelons.

In this neighborhood there were two barbershops: one union, one nonunion. Haircuts were 25 cents at the union shop and only 15 cents at the nonunion establishment. These shops also offered shaves and shoeshines for 10 cents. Occasionally, if one of the shoeshine boys got low on cash, he would make a personal call at someone's home and ask to shine their shoes.

Considering all the economic stress during the Depression, the amazing thing about this small district was every business survived at that time. But as of this writing, only one furniture store is still in operation. Sadly, the rest exist only in memory.

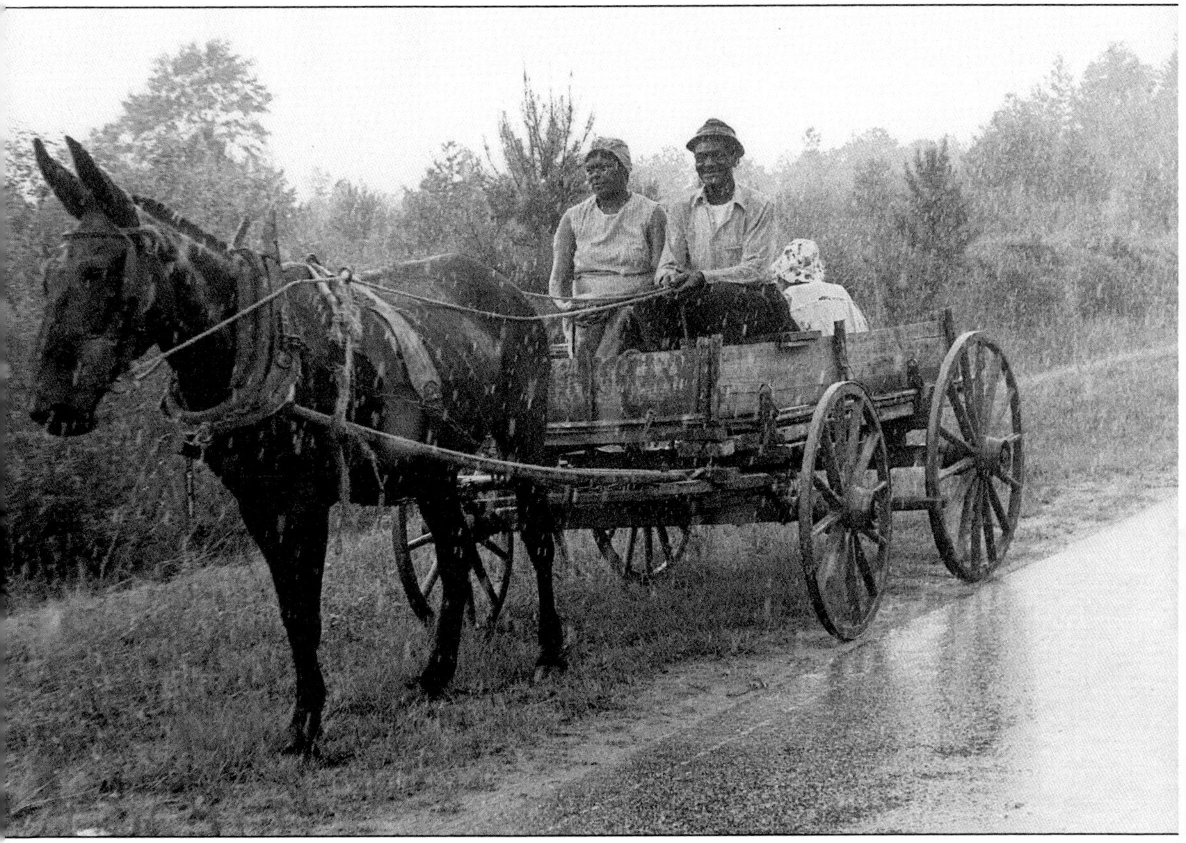

A mule-drawn wagon was the way most peddlers got their produce to market during the Depression years.

Peddlers and Curb Markets

In the days before large grocery stores supplied almost every need, country peddlers were a common sight in most small towns in the South. This was especially true in the spring and summer, when they could be seen on the street or around the courthouse square selling fresh produce from their farms.

Since it was a simpler era, most of the peddlers came to town in mule-drawn wagons, because only a few owned trucks. In the back of their wagons would be the goods they had for sale, such as corn, beans, peas, okra, tomatoes, turnip greens, or cabbage.

No one peddler would have every item needed by a household, so while one might offer primarily vegetables, another would have eggs, chicken, butter, and buttermilk; and still another would only be selling watermelons.

When he was on the road, the peddler had a particular route and tried to maintain a schedule for his customers. Upon his arrival, the women would examine his produce to see if it fit in with their schedule of meals.

The appearance of a peddler served a secondary function beyond providing food; it brought the neighborhood women together around his wagon, where they could also exchange news. Sometimes the women would continue to talk, long after the peddler left.

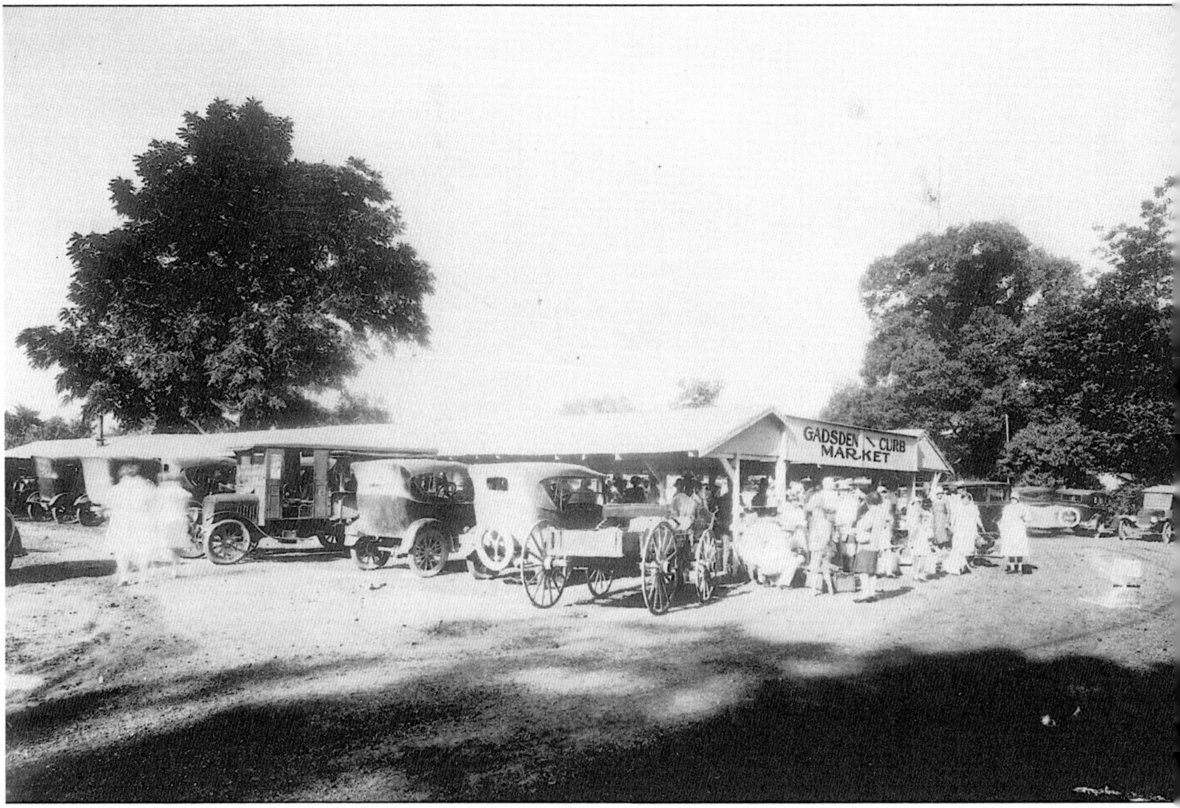

The Curb Market, located at the corner of Chestnut and Eighth Street, was another place a peddler could sell his produce.

Being independent businessmen, these peddlers sold to more than one source. Not only did they deal with individual customers, but they were a major supplier for the grocery stores.

The curb market was another venue where the peddler could sell his products. The curb market, known also as a "farmer's market," and the peddler both shared a common goal, which was to sell their produce. However, they did this in opposite ways: the peddler took his wares to the customer, whereas the customer came to the curb market between established hours.

The life of a peddler was hard and most of them had a long route that kept them moving from sun-up to sun-down. As they traveled by wagon, it was a slow process and some of them—depending on where they lived—would leave home before daylight. Each peddler knew how long it would take to run his route, so in the afternoon he would leave town just in time to arrive home before dark.

This could work to the advantage of some customers. At the end of his route, when the peddler was tired, was apparently the best time to get a good deal. Facing a long trip home, he would be quick to reduce a price; the peddler had no desire to take his produce back to the farm.

The peddler was a very important part of small town life in the South during the Depression. With the coming of large grocery stores, and then supermarkets, the peddler quickly became an extinct breed. Today, a peddler lives only in the memory of his loyal customers, who depended on his services during the hard times of the 1930s.

The Home Place

In 1930, my father's family moved in with his grandmother after the death of her husband. It was in this house that my father spent the decade of the 1930s, growing from a 10-year-old child into a young college student.

Looking at this house today, which is still standing in the exact same location in the old neighborhood, it is hard to believe the amount of activity that occurred on a 50 x 200-foot city lot.

The house itself faced south, and at its front corner stood a pecan tree. In the backyard, at the back door, was a rose arbor with a swing under it.

On the west side of the house a driveway led back to the garage. About halfway down the driveway was a fig tree; just past it grew a couple of stalks of poke salad, which was frequently mixed in and cooked with other greens.

The garage served as a multi-purpose building with a work area at the back and included a coal and storage shed on the side. Behind the garage was the chicken yard and farther behind it was the cow lot; a small barn stood on the edge of the property.

While all of this was on the west half of the backyard, the east side equally satisfied a functional purpose. Across from the garage, and extending to the end of the lot, was the family garden. Also on this side, between the house and the garden, was the wash place where my father's mother washed the family's clothes by hand under the Chinaberry tree.

During those lean years everyone in the family helped out in their own way, even the children. For my father, his chores around the house included keeping the coal scuttles filled during the winter, feeding the chickens, keeping the grass mowed during the summer (with a reel-type push mower), as well as providing water for and taking the cow to pasture to graze.

With times so difficult during the Depression, it was essential for a family to utilize all the resources at their command. For this one family, though "city dwellers," it meant operating their small backyard almost as if it were a farm, producing whatever necessities they could to ease their economic burden. In working together, and making the most of what they had, the family was able to survive the Depression.

Heating Systems

When my father was young in the 1930s, the heating system at his house included one laundry heater in the kitchen and three coal burning fireplaces. The fireplaces were located in the living room and in the middle and back bedrooms.

Since the living room was only used for special occasions, a fire was rarely burned there. It was the middle bedroom, which also doubled as a sitting room, that was kept warm because it was the actual living space for the family.

"We later got a Heatrola for the middle bedroom, which replaced the fireplace," my father recalled. "While the Heatrola was a vast improvement over the fireplace, it really was nothing more than a potbellied stove encased in sheet metal with a wood grain finish."

The Heatrola put out much more heat than the inefficient fireplace because it sat in front of the hearth and projected its warmth into the whole room. However, it was not capable of heating more than a limited area.

"My room was the back bedroom and it was never heated," my father said. "It was on the north side of the house and in the winter felt like an icebox!"

Before the days of efficient heating and cooling, weather extremes in a house were a fact of life people had to contend with in whatever manner they could.

"I slept on a feather bed with a 'double blanket' that was folded over like a sleeping bag. My bed had so much cover on it for warmth I could barely turn over," my father said. "Then a hot water bottle was placed at my feet in an effort to keep them warm. Winter nights in that back bedroom are not nights I would like to relive. It was almost like sleeping outdoors."

Such was life in the times before houses were well insulated and effective air-conditioning and heating provided real relief from the weather. In those days, before a house became its own temperate environment regardless of the season, nature ruled supreme. The best most people could hope for was a change in the natural weather—either warmer in winter or cooler in summer.

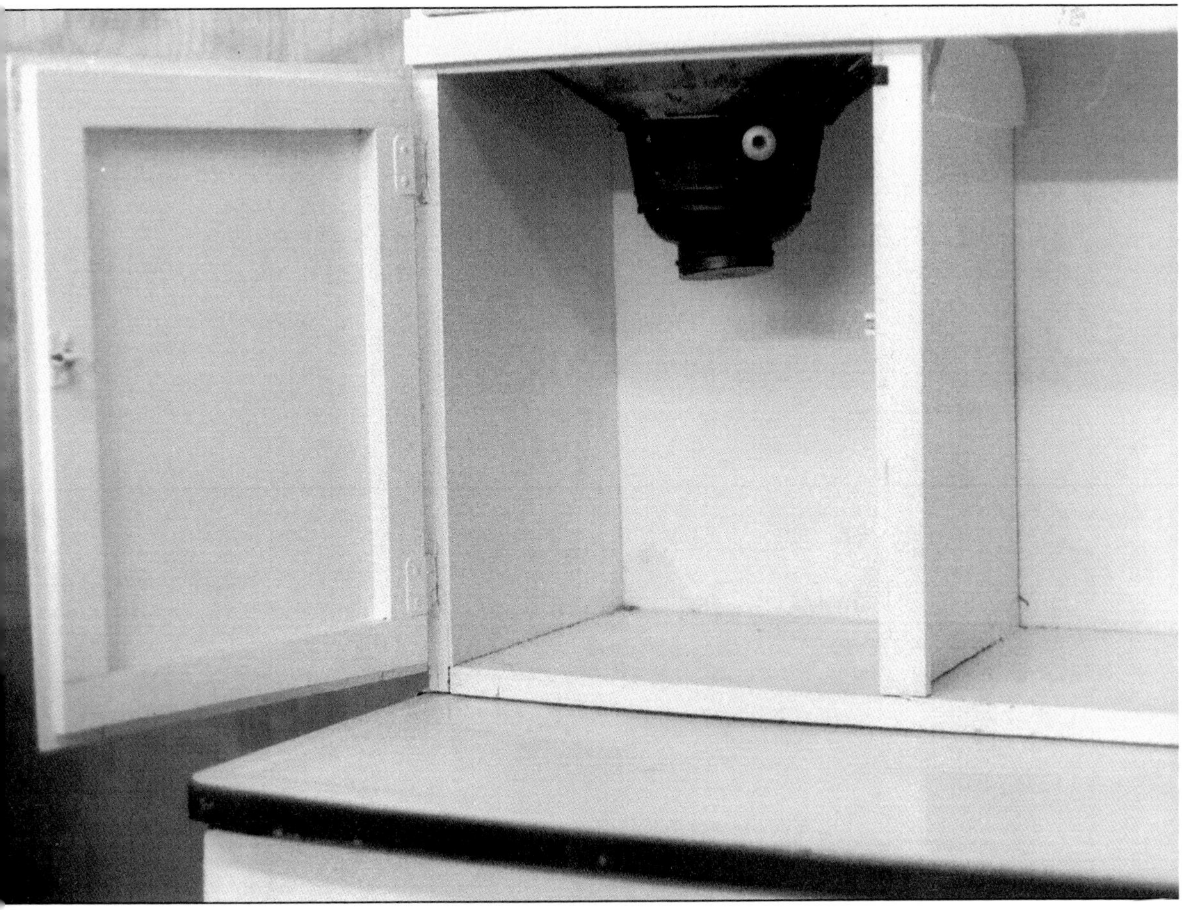

This flour sifter sits inside a kitchen cabinet of the 1930s.

The Kitchen

By today's standards, the kitchen of the 1930s was a primitive arrangement.

"Mother was fortunate enough to have an electric stove that stood on four legs like a table, with an oven attached to the left side," my father recalled. "It didn't have a timer or any automatic controls, but it was far superior to a wood, kerosene, or coal burning unit."

His mother's kitchen, at the beginning of the 1930s, also contained an icebox. It was small and didn't keep its contents very cold.

For that reason, the milk was always placed in the top next to the ice. As the ice melted it ran down a tube into the drip pan beneath the icebox and, if it wasn't emptied frequently, would overflow.

When the pan overflowed, a small stream of water could be seen coming from under the icebox. Then as the pan was pulled out a bigger mess was made, as even more water sloshed out.

About twice a week the iceman would supply the family with a block of ice. As he approached, there was a bell on his truck he would clang to let his customers know he was near.

A family would then quickly check their supply to determine how much ice they needed. Someone would holler out to the iceman for "a nickel's or a dime's worth."

The amount of ice varied from time to time, depending on how hot the weather

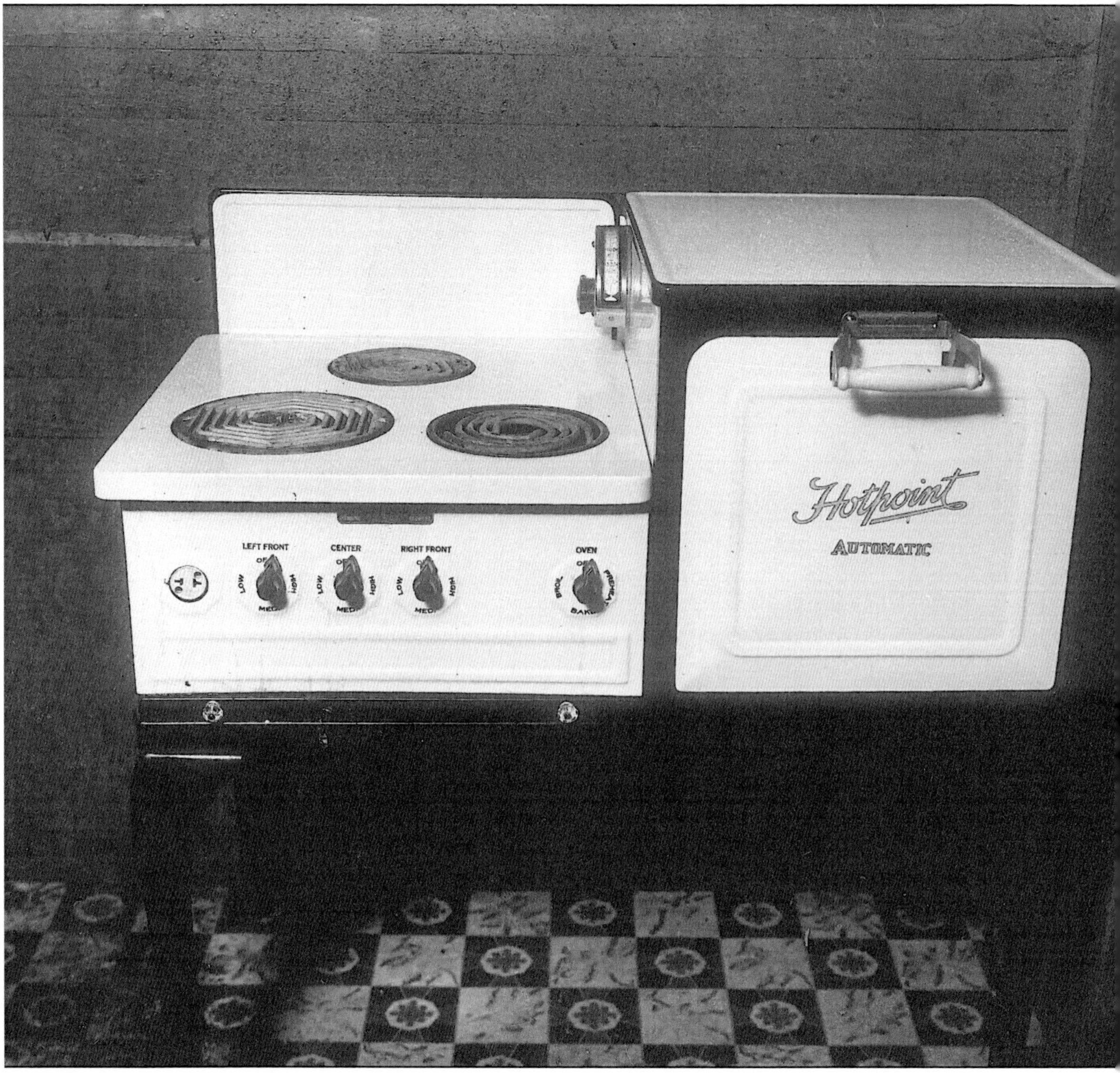

A Hotpoint stove of the 1930s was a big improvement over coal, wood-burning, or kerosene stoves.

was, how many times the icebox was opened, and how much ice had been chipped off for iced tea and cold water.

In the back of the truck were large blocks of ice and the iceman would chip off whatever amount his customers needed.

The coming of the ice truck surprisingly served another purpose. It became a signal for the neighborhood kids to come running, because sometimes the iceman would give them a small piece of ice to eat.

Another necessity in the kitchen was a cabinet with a small working area off to the side, used in mixing dough for biscuits, cakes, and cornbread. Inside, behind swinging doors, was a storage space for meal and spices; as well as a separate compartment for flour, which included a sifter.

Sitting in a back corner of the kitchen, a coal burning laundry heater provided hot, running water. Due to the extra heat

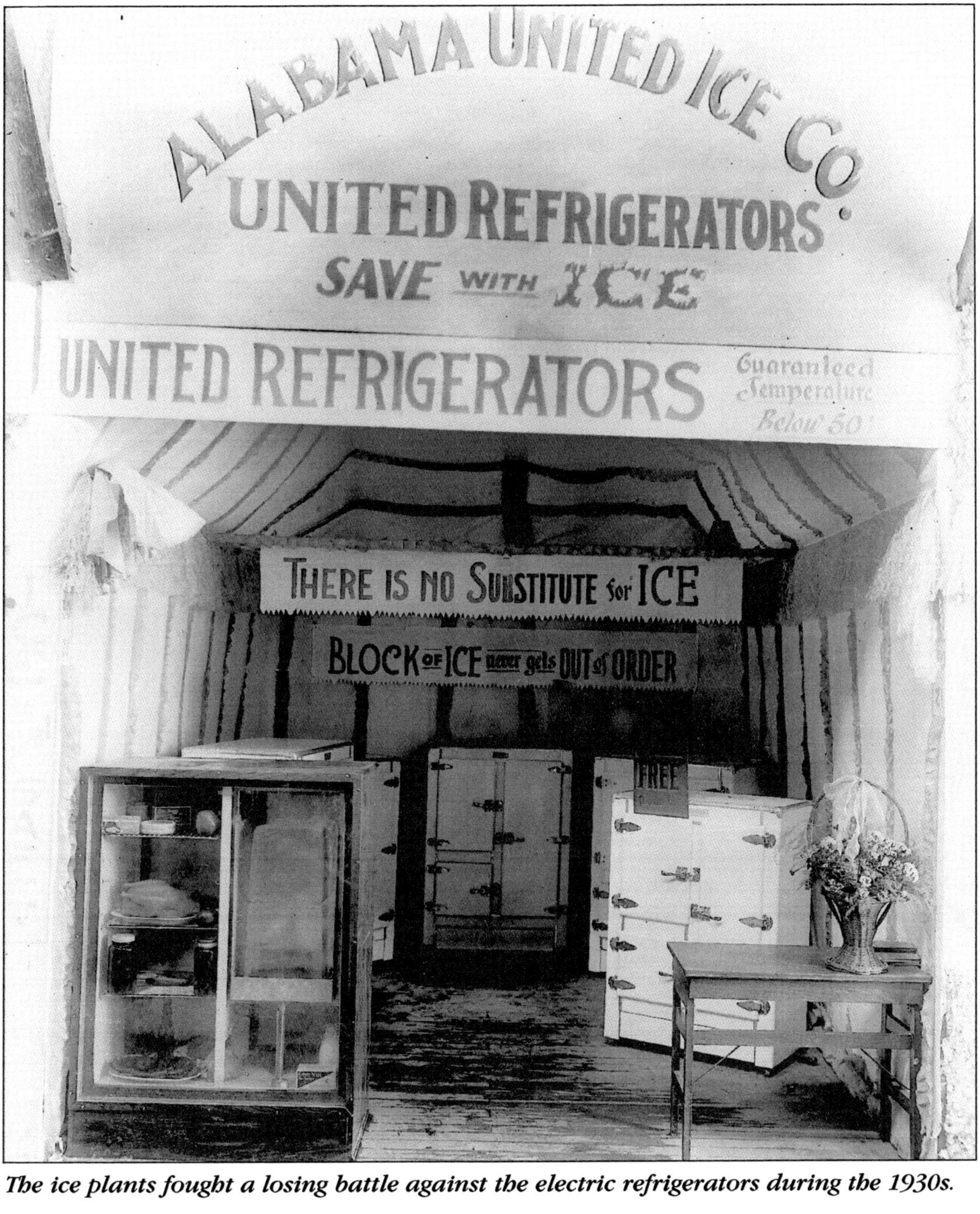

The ice plants fought a losing battle against the electric refrigerators during the 1930s.

it provided, the heater was only used until noon.

It was nice to have hot water, but it wasn't so nice for a woman to work in the kitchen in summer with a fire going in the heater.

Although cooking was the main activity in the kitchen, it was also where the family took their meals. When my father sat at the table, his back faced the heater. This was great in winter, but extremely hot during the summer.

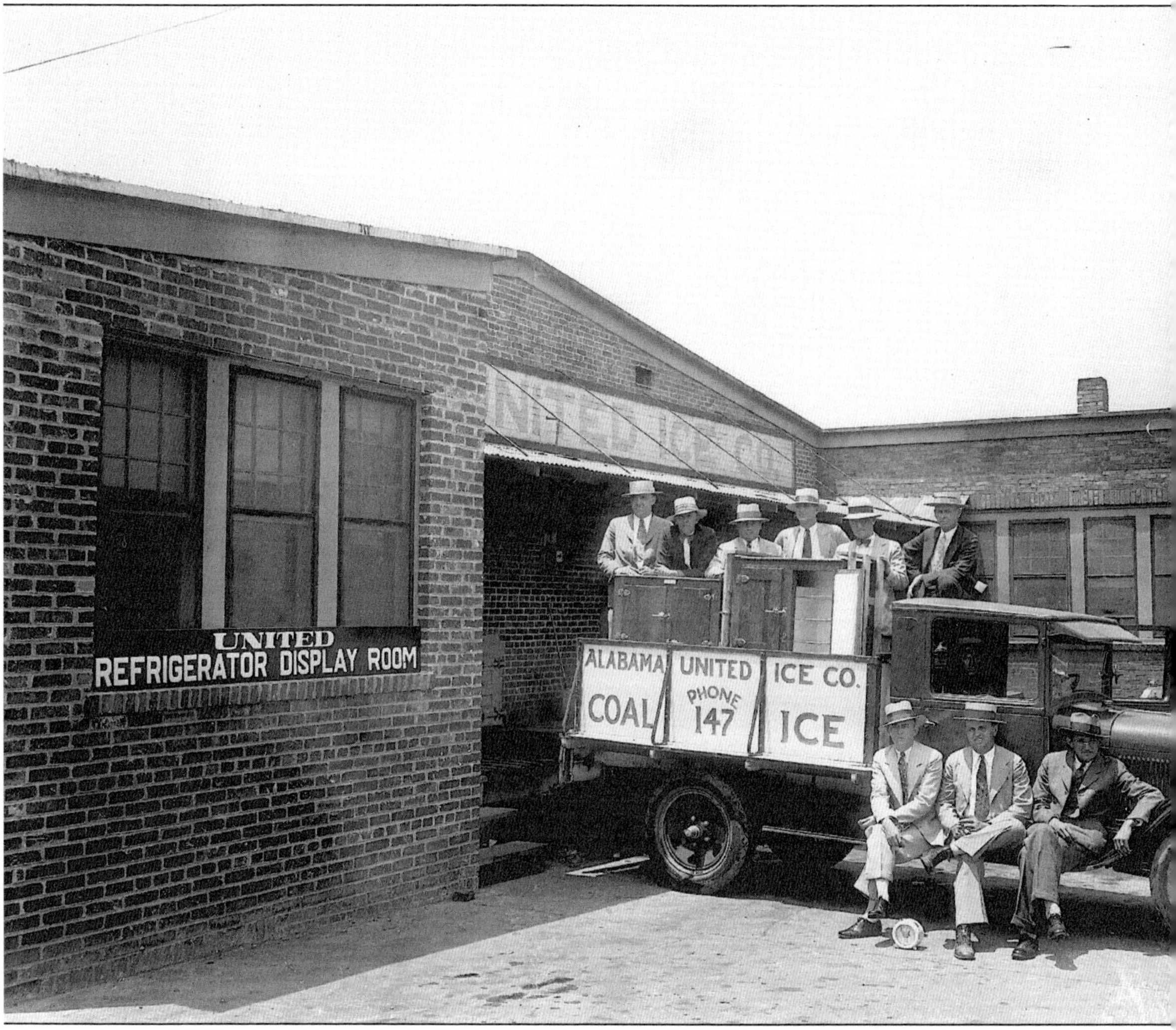

The ice truck came about twice a week and the iceman would chip off whatever amount his customers needed.

Looking back, the Depression was hard on everybody; but it was especially difficult for women. With very few conveniences in the kitchen, they prepared meals on antiquated equipment and under less-than-ideal working conditions.

Depression Food

The meals of the 1930s consisted of simple fare. They regularly included such staples as dried beans, turnip greens, cornbread and potatoes. Often it all would be washed down with cold buttermilk.

Because the cost of meat was so high, it was seldom found on most tables. Occasionally, though, "sow belly" or pork was served. When it was, this white meat would be thinly sliced and fried.

It went perfectly with greens or cornbread and was sometimes called "bumpy bacon."

If a family kept a garden, the first vegetables to "come in" would be lettuce, onions, and radishes. As a fresh salad, some favored these ingredients mixed together with white meat grease poured over them as a dressing.

Sandwiches were popular during the Depression but, unlike today, had to be made from "scratch" because very few ingredients were prepackaged. At that time, boiled ham was one of the few prepackaged items on the market.

A potato sandwich is a good example of a Depression-era, homemade meal. A potato would be sliced, then fried in deep grease. Plenty of mayonnaise was spread on one piece of bread while the fried potatoes placed on the other. When put together, it was one delicious, homemade taste treat!

Naturally, this was in the good old days before everyone became obsessed about calories and cholesterol.

Another sandwich common then was pimento cheese. Like the others, pimento cheese did not come from a store but was made at home by cutting and mixing "hoop" cheese and pimentos from a jar.

For supper during the Depression, most meals were the leftovers from lunch. If these were needed for the next day, the meal might be simply cornbread and sweet milk, or cornbread and buttermilk. To enhance the flavor of this simple meal, an onion would occasionally be added to the buttermilk and cornbread.

The Depression was a hard time and families were struggling just to get by. The meals from that era reflected this austerity, with simple but hardy fare.

For the people who grew up under these conditions, eating Depression-era meals such as milk and bread, the variety of food available today is a wonder to behold. But for some, there is nothing that can beat the old-fashioned taste of cold buttermilk and cornbread.

Chicken Dinner

Times were hard during the Depression, so a chicken dinner was a delicacy reserved for special occasions: either Sunday guests or a visiting preacher.

During the 1930s, there were three ways a chicken might be obtained. The first was from a grocery store; the second from a peddler; and the third was one you had raised yourself.

Regardless of the source, all the chickens would be live. If they came from a store they were not plucked and cut up for cooking, but living in a coop. When it came time to select a chicken, the lady of the house would reach in and feel the breast, to see how much meat it had.

Sometimes she couldn't find one that was suitable for cooking that day, so she would buy it, bring it home, and put it in a coop. After feeding it for a few days, it would be the right sizc to kill.

Special skills were required to bring a chicken home from the store. First, its legs would be tied together; then a hole would be torn in one corner of a sack, with the chicken's head placed through the hole. Finally the lady would be ready to carry the chicken home by the legs, its body stuck in the sack to minimize flapping from its wings.

Once the chicken was home, the next step would be in preparing it for cooking. The first thing to do was kill it, which was done by either wringing its neck or taking an axe and cutting the head off. After this, the chicken would be dipped in a pot of scalding water to soften the feathers, so they could be plucked.

When the larger feathers were plucked, the cook would take a loosely rolled newspaper and set one end on fire, going

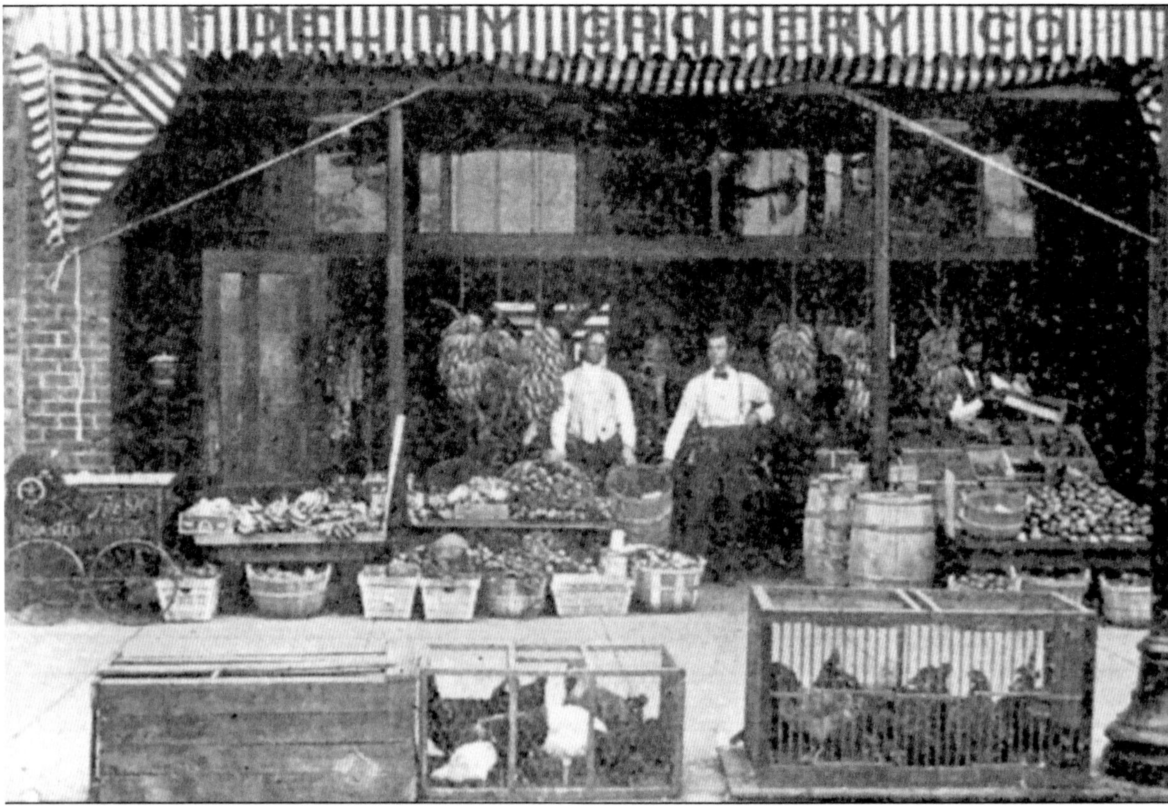

During the 1930s, chickens were kept in a coop in front of the store. The cook could then reach in to select the perfect bird for a chicken dinner.

all over the chicken to singe off the feathers that were too small to hand-pluck.

If it was a fryer, the chicken had to be dressed and cut into different pieces: the legs, breast, thighs and wings. Now it was ready to be cooked (fried in lard), which was always done in a black, cast-iron skillet.

With all the work finished, everyone was eager to sit down to a delicious meal. Spring and summer meals would be fried chicken, and in winter it would be baked chicken and dressing.

Accompanying the main course would be hot biscuits, fried okra, chicken gravy, green beans, mashed potatoes, and good conversation—all over the hardy, homecooked meal prepared specially as only a mother knew how.

Wash Day

With the old order seemingly falling apart, even during the depths of the Depression, some things remained the same. At my father's house during the 1930s, every Monday was wash day.

In their backyard was a Chinaberry tree and under this tree was his mother's wash place. It was nothing more than a raised platform with three wash tubs sitting on it, so she wouldn't have to bend over constantly to reach her work.

On the ground, in front of this platform, sat a wooden grate for her to stand on in case the yard was muddy.

"On Monday, wash day, my dad would first build a fire under the wash pot and fill it with water," my father said. "When

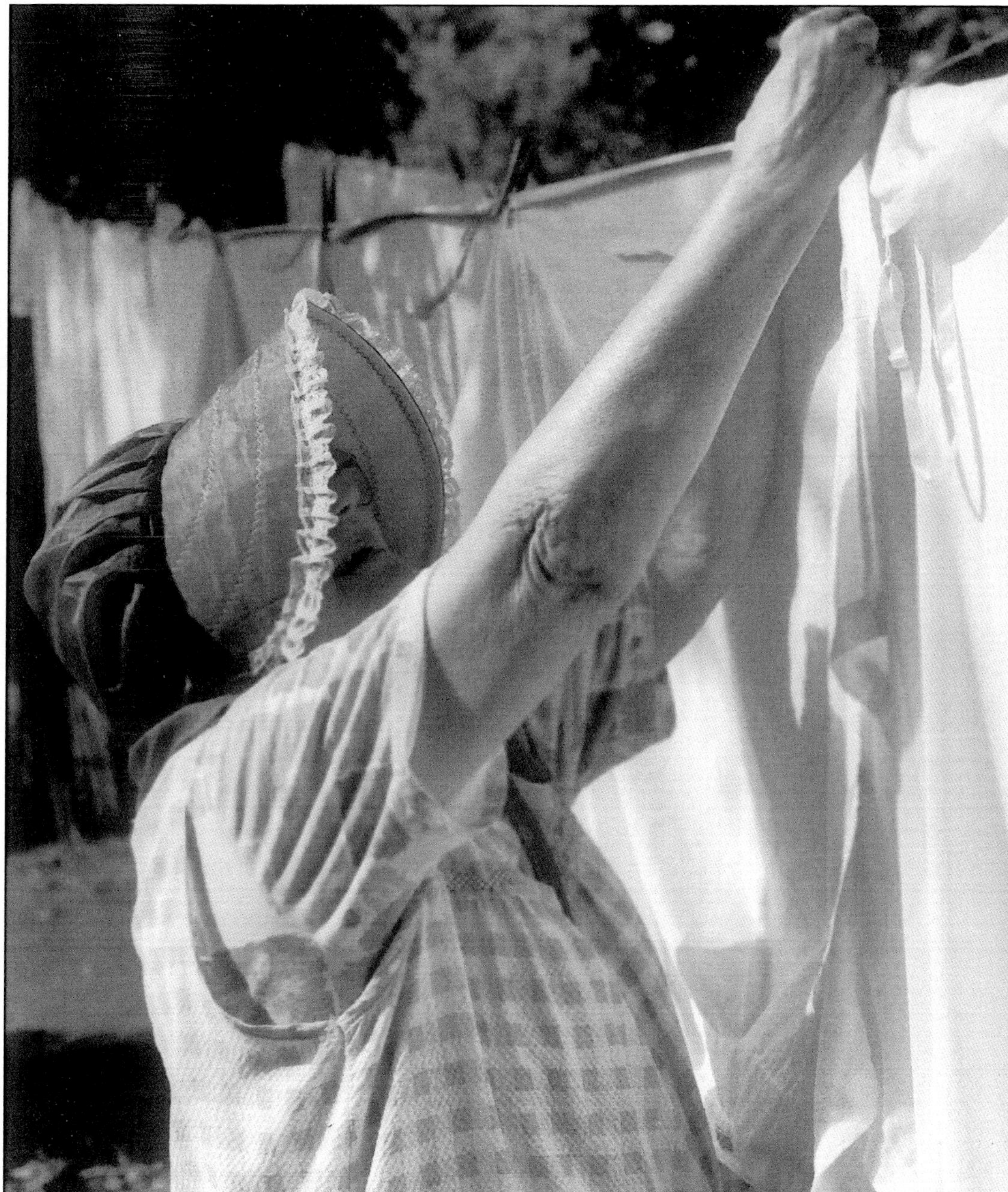

Before dryers, women hung their clothes on a line. Nothing smelled as good as sun-dried, fresh clothes.

mother finished breakfast, she would go outside and shave Octagon soap into the pot."

Once the water came to a rolling boil the dirty clothes would be placed in the wash pot. When the clothes had boiled for a time, they would be lifted out with a stick and placed into the first tub of water, which had a rub board in it. After they were washed and scrubbed to satisfaction, the clothes would be moved to the second tub for rinsing.

After this, the clothes would be placed into a third tub for the final rinse. In this tub was "blueing," which was a bright blue powder. It came out of a wooden cylinder six-inches long, with holes in one end for sifting out the contents.

Blueing was put into the water to make the colors in the clothes brighter. When this task was completed, the clean clothes were hung on the line to dry.

The clothes line was strung between two fence posts, at opposite ends of the yard. Since the clothes were wet, the line had a tendency to sag and a prop was needed under them to prevent the clothes from dragging the ground.

Washing clothes was not an easy task for the women of the Depression era, but it was a job that had to be done regardless of bad weather or time of the year.

During the Depression, there were always tasks to perform around the home. But for one woman, my grandmother, every Monday was wash day. It was a ritual she observed religiously unless extreme weather kept her indoors.

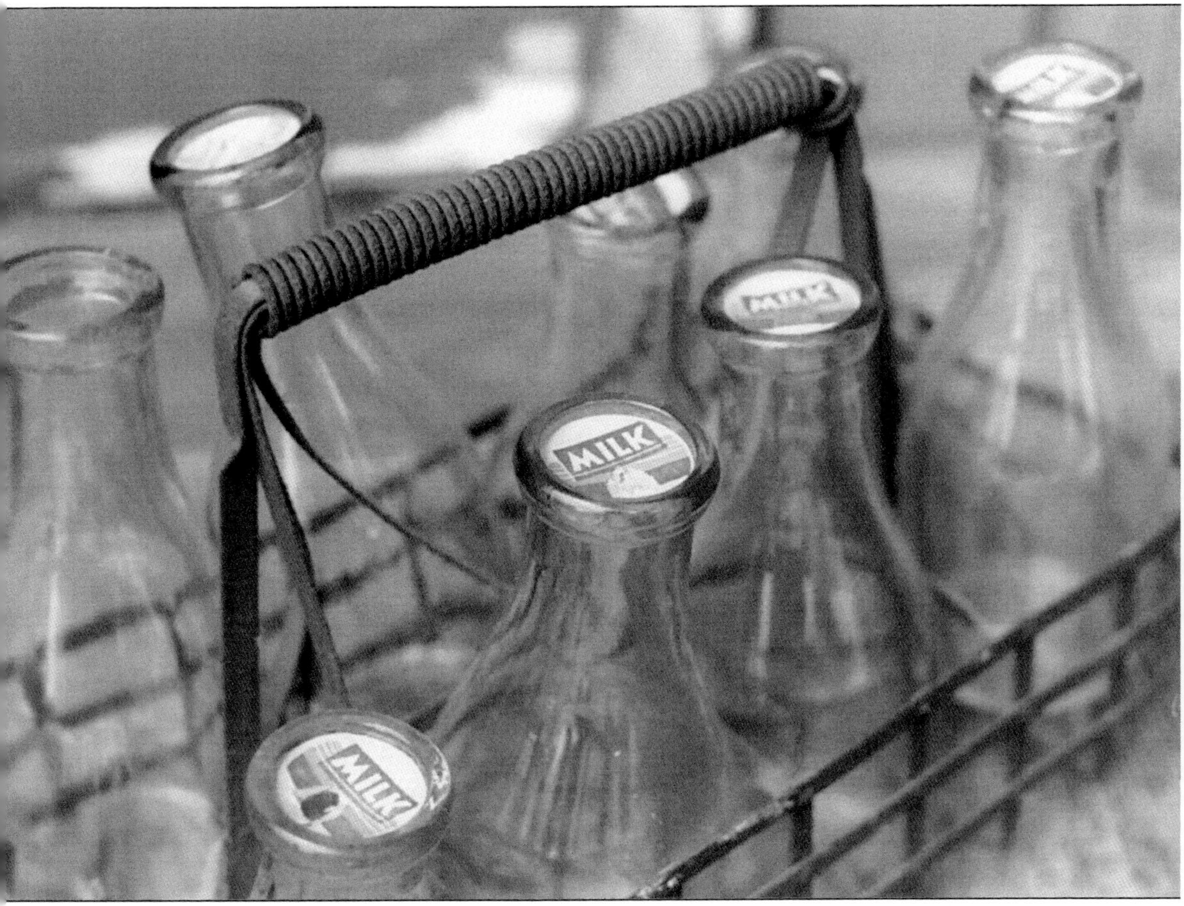

On cold mornings, the milk would would freeze, pushing the stopper up. The frozen cream at the top could then be broken off and eaten.

Milk

At one time in America's past, most towns had a number of local dairies that supplied milk. The milk was delivered directly to the homes in a glass bottle with a cardboard stopper in the top.

After the family emptied a bottle, it would be washed and placed on the front porch. When the milkman made his next delivery, he would pick up the empty bottles and take them back to the dairy.

Usually there was a set amount of milk delivered to each house. Although if the family needed a different amount, some whipping cream or butter, a note would be placed in an empty bottle and the delivery man would follow the instructions.

During these years, the milk was not homogenized, so the thicker cream separated from the milk. To use it the milk had to be stirred, so the cream would blend in.

The children were happiest on cold days when the milk would freeze. If this happened, it would push the stopper up and a piece of this frozen milk could be broken off and eaten. This popsicle was nothing but pure, rich cream.

Of course, this wasn't too pleasing to the mothers. If the children ate all the cream, they were left with only skim milk!

"During the 1930s I had an uncle who died, leaving my aunt with four children and no way to make a living," my father said. "About this time my dad thought it would be a good idea to get a cow."

"My mother didn't know how to milk a cow but my aunt did. So the idea was for my family to buy and feed the cow, while my aunt would handle the milking duties. That way, both families could have milk."

At that time it was legal to keep a cow in the city. With a number of people keeping animals, the owners of some lots would fence in their property and rent it out as pastureland.

"It became my job to take the cow to pasture," my father remembered, "and then, late in the afternoon, to return and bring her home."

"In the summer, the pasture might be overgrazed or so dry there would not be a sufficient amount of grass. My dad solved this problem by having me take our cow and stake it out on some vacant lot with plenty of dry grass. However, our cow was so stupid she would get tangled up in the rope and I would have to untangle her legs several times a day."

At that time, the alleys behind the houses in town were never mowed so the grass was high and lush.

"Unfortunately, I had to stay with our cow while she was grazing in the alley," my father said, "while all the other boys were playing ball or going swimming. And here I was, holding a rope with a stupid cow attached to the other end!"

This cow interfered with my father's life during his growing up years and he claims his disdain for the beast endures to this day.

"When my dad finally decided to sell this cow, which we called 'Hannah,' and go back to getting milk from the dairy, it was a great day of celebration for me."

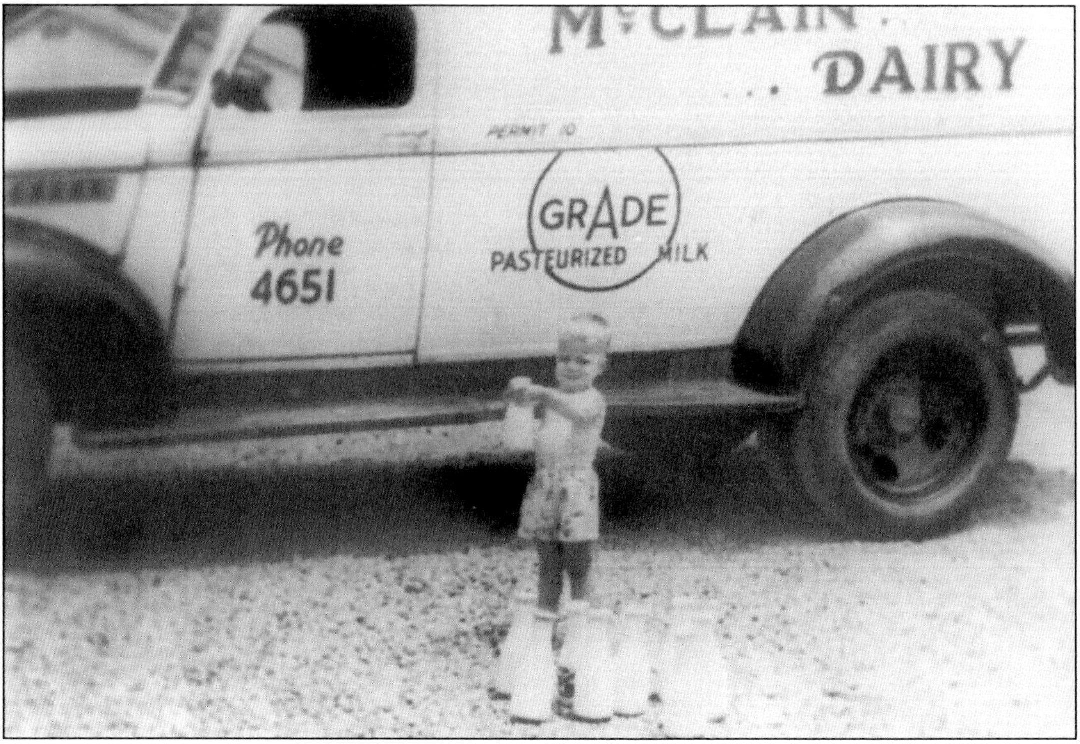

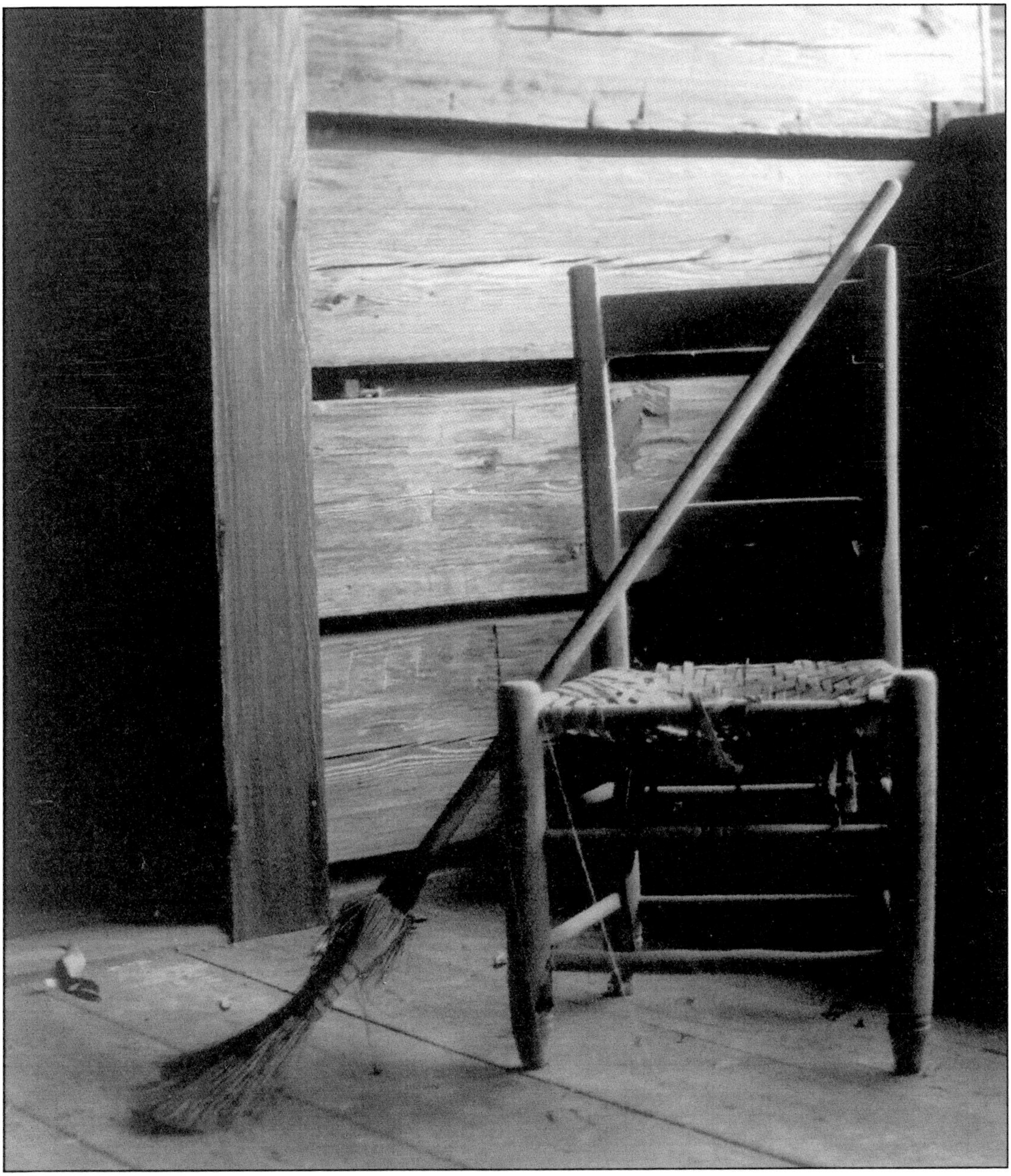

Women were the real heroes of the Depression. Even though a broom rests against a chair, a woman's work was never done.

THE FAMILY

No one escaped the hardships brought about by the Depression. While the women labored at home with household duties, most of the men were either without jobs or on short-time schedules. Because they couldn't earn enough money to provide for their families, the sense of personal failure took a heavy emotional toll on family life at that time.

The children also suffered. Many didn't have proper clothes and came to school hungry; and, during the Depression, there were no governmental programs for breakfast or lunch at school.

The people who suffered most were the wives and mothers. It became their responsibility to manage what little money was available and to provide the necessities of life for the entire family.

But a woman's responsibilities didn't stop there; in addition, she cooked all meals, washed and ironed the family's clothes, and cleaned the house. If there was a sick, disabled or bedridden member of the family, the job of caring for this person also became her duty.

At a time when everyone was suffering through the Depression, families had to pull together and rely on each other for support. Although each member played his part, make no mistake about it—the women were the real heroes of the Depression years.

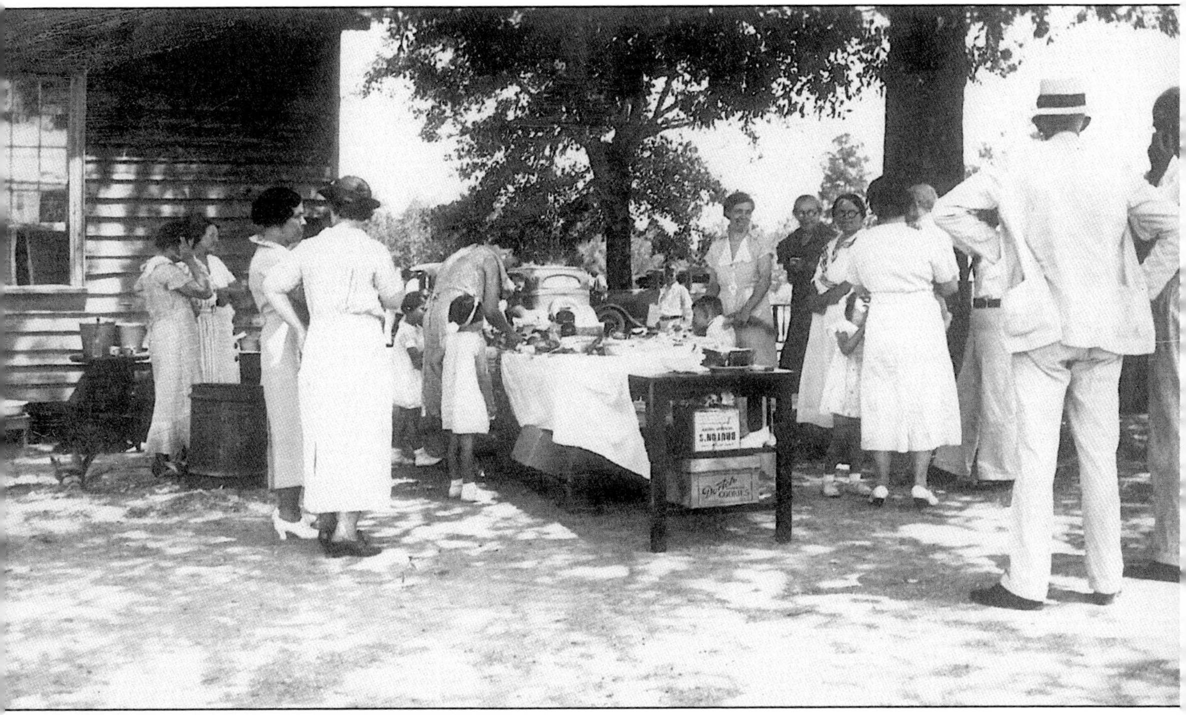

Church picnics were a popular pastime during the hard years of the Depression era.

CHURCH

With the country in turmoil during the Depression, the neighborhood churches played an important role in the lives of the people; not only spiritually, but socially as well.

Practically everyone in the neighborhood attended either the Methodist, Baptist, or Presbyterian church. These churches were centrally located in the community and most people walked to the services since they didn't have automobiles or were trying to save money on gasoline.

Church life filled a social need by having suppers, Sunday school parties, hikes, Easter egg hunts, and wiener roasts; some even sponsored Boy Scout troops.

During the Depression, most churches were having a difficult time financially due to the severe economic conditions. Therefore, shortly before the preacher's salary was due the church board held what was called a "hide and tallow" meeting.

At this meeting each board member was given a list of members to contact. The purpose behind the "hide and tallow" meeting was to strongly encourage those on the list to donate operating funds for the church.

The board members would then go to each person's home on their list and explain the situation. They would ask for a donation and would be lucky if they received 25 or 50 cents.

There was one member of the church who owned a drug store. While this man never attended church, every time he was approached about a contribution he would make a $5 donation, which was a lot of money during the Depression.

Most churches of that time were heated by potbellied stoves. Since there were no assistants, it was the preacher's responsibility to build a fire on Sunday morning. My father tells about one such preacher who was completely baldheaded and, at times, could be seen in

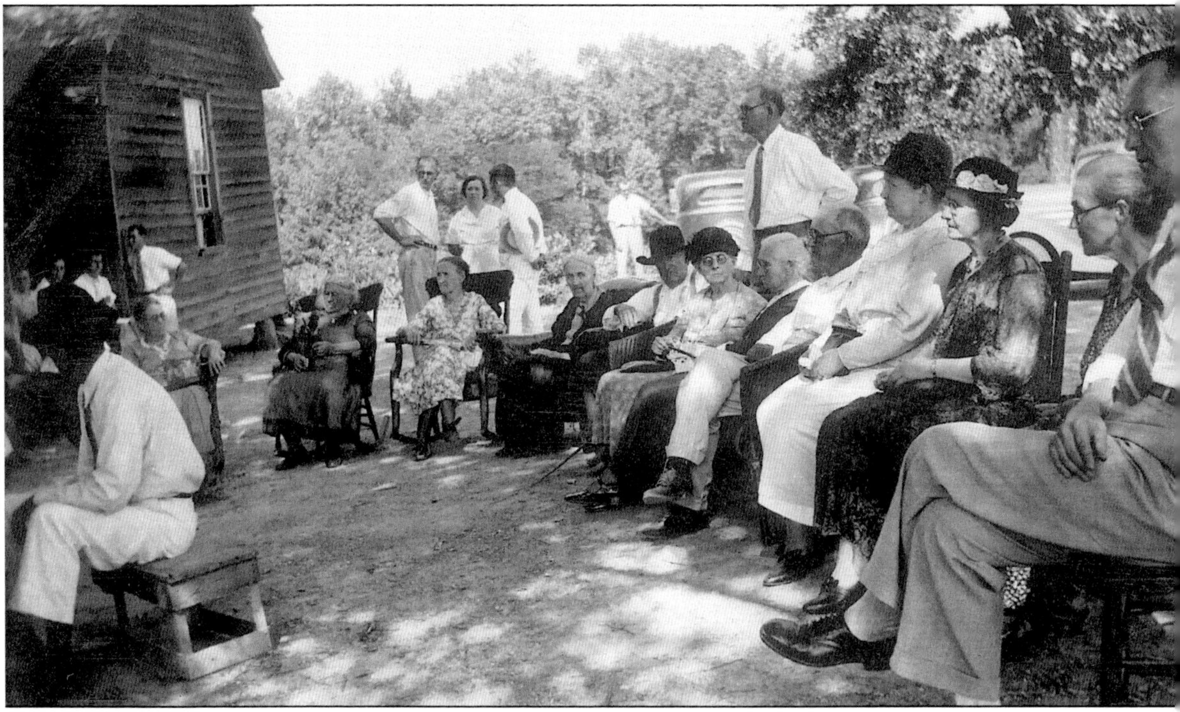

These people enjoy the fellowship of a church social event, c. 1935.

the pulpit with soot spots on his head.

Because of hot weather in the summer, churches would occasionally hold tent revivals. The congregation looked forward to these services because they could meet in relative comfort and enjoy each other socially, as well as receive spiritual inspiration.

All through the lean times of the 1930s, the church became a steadying influence and a bulwark for a people who had lost so much, and had only their hopes of a better future to look forward to. In this climate, the church truly fulfilled its mission as the Rock of Ages.

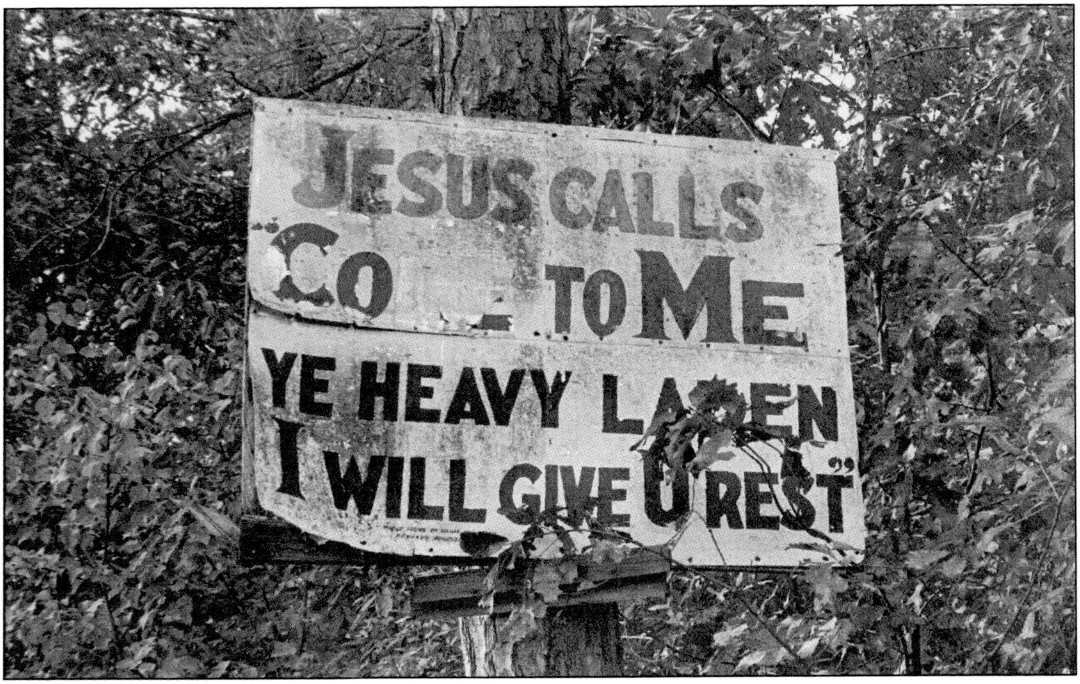

Religious signs were frequently seen on the roadways of the Deep South during the trying years of the Depression.

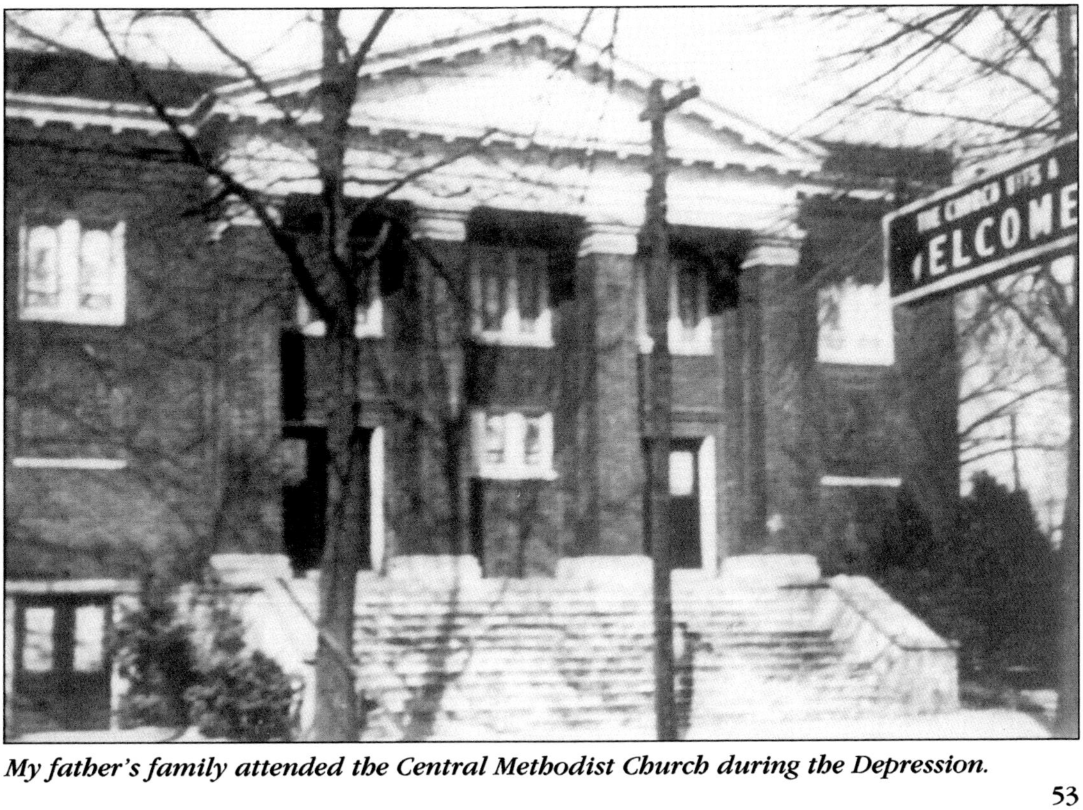

My father's family attended the Central Methodist Church during the Depression.

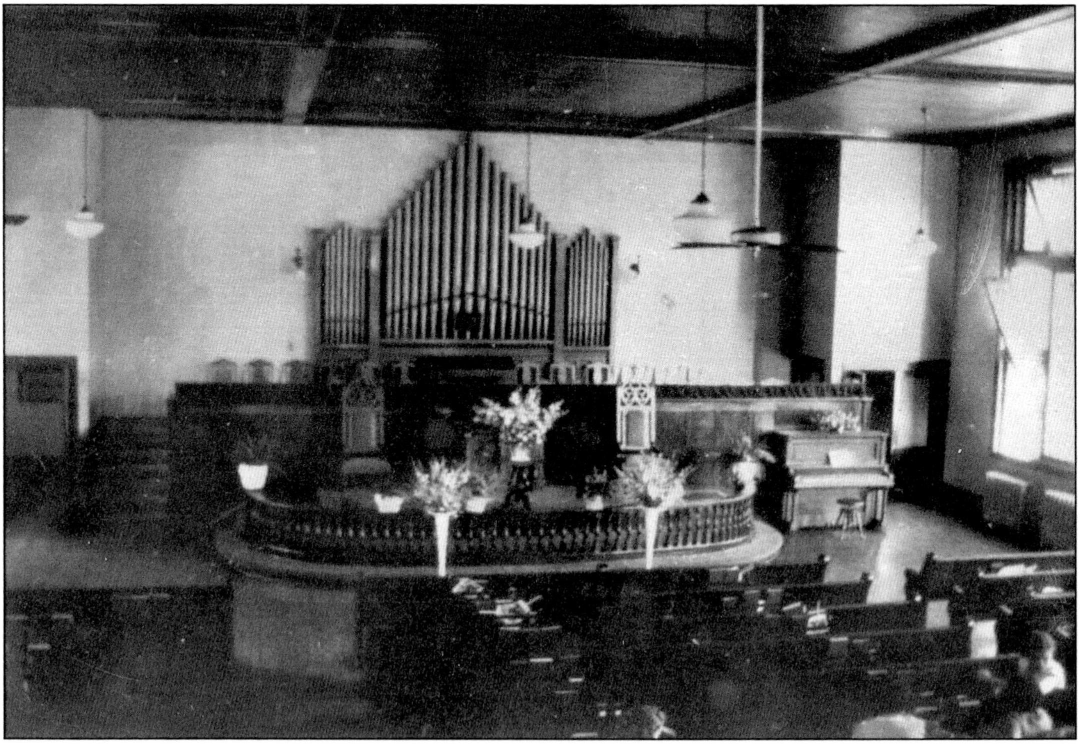

The inside of the Central Methodist Church can be seen in this 1930s photograph.

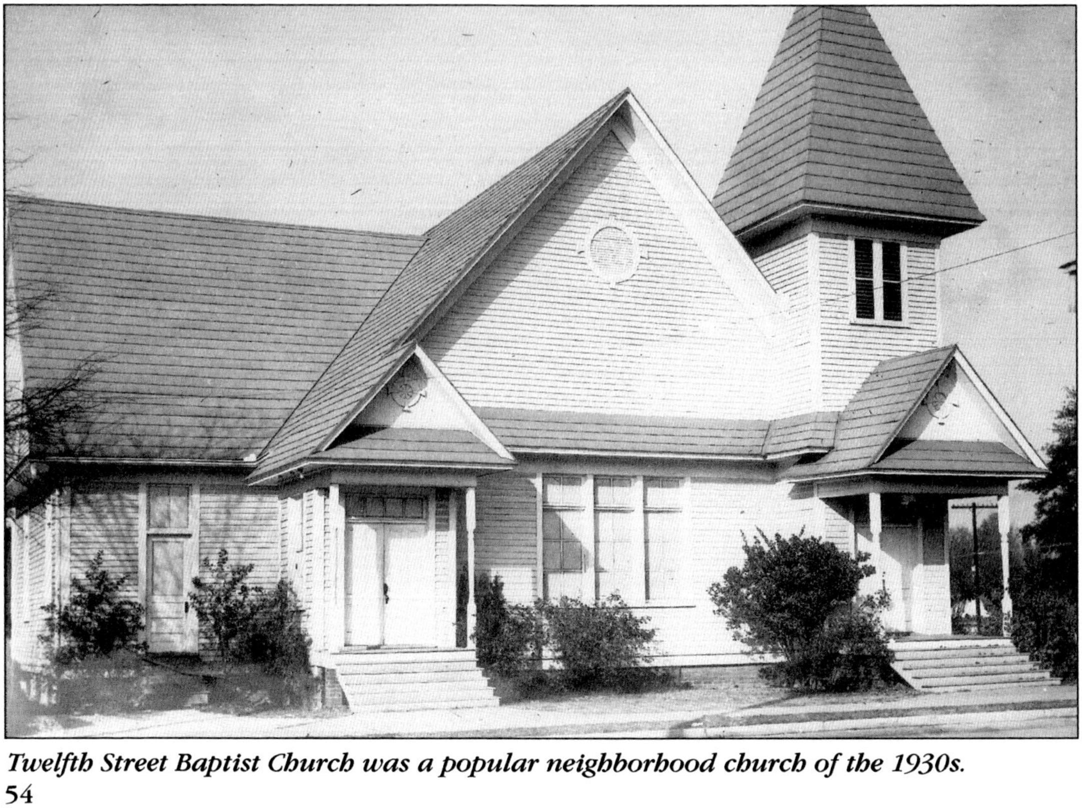

Twelfth Street Baptist Church was a popular neighborhood church of the 1930s.

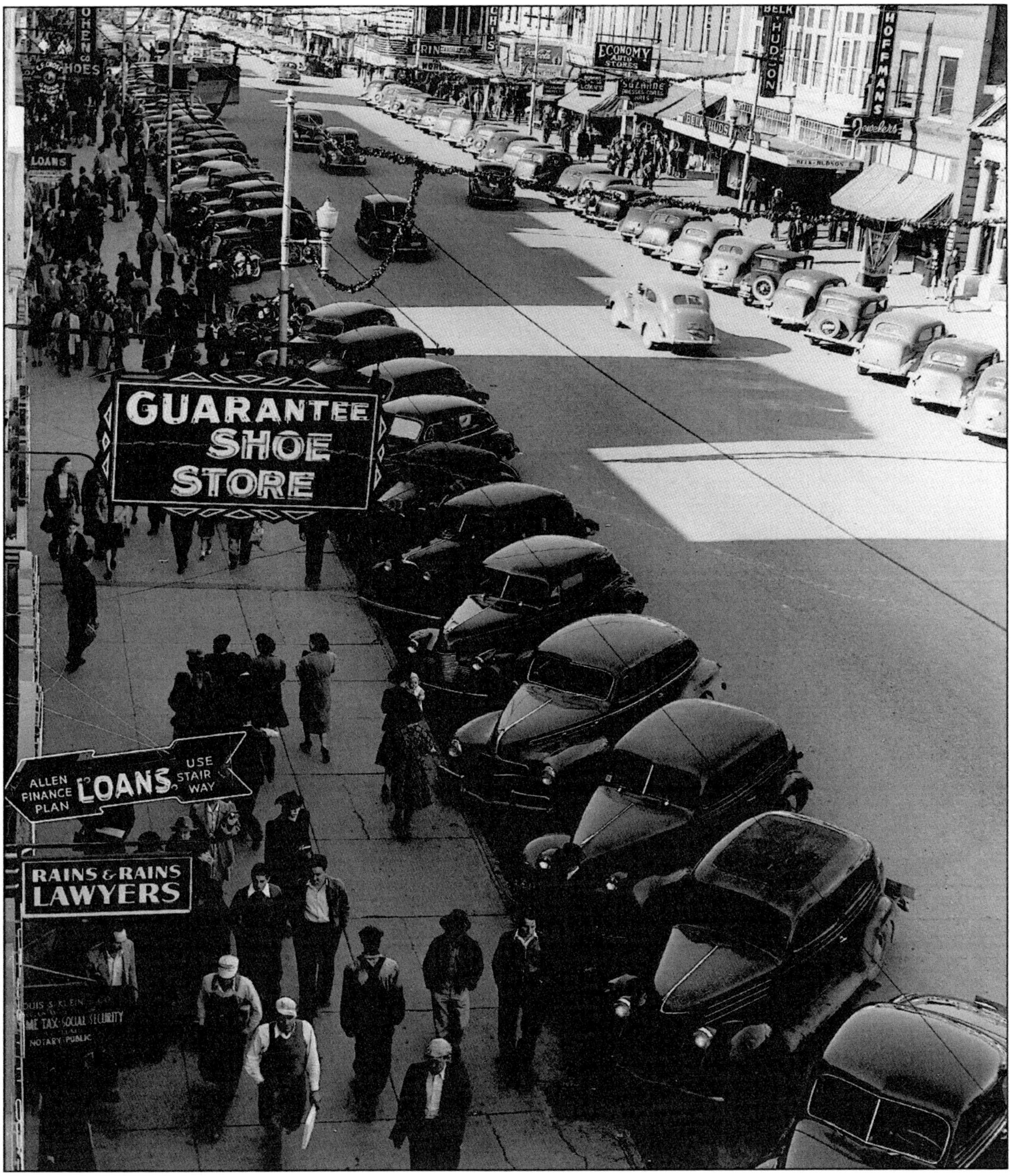

Gadsden was always crowded during the Christmas season with shoppers on the street and people going in and out of stores. My father is walking next to the man with the "G" sweater. (Photograph courtesy of Library of Congress.)

CHRISTMAS

Although times were hard, Christmas was still eagerly anticipated by children during the Depression. Regardless of the economic climate, it was a time of special joy and celebration with candy, nuts and fruit to accompany the added holiday cheer. For most people, Christmas meant presents under a freshly cut, decorated tree and a big Christmas dinner.

As the time drew near, the holiday season officially began when a family member went into the woods and selected the "perfect" tree, which was always a native grown cedar. Then it would be cut down and hauled back to the house, where the entire family would help decorate it with bright lights, shiny ornaments, tinsel and icicles. Once this task had been accomplished, and everyone stepped back to admire their efforts, the Christmas season was in full swing.

Part of the fun and excitement of the holiday season was shopping. Christmas shopping was an adventure because, in the 1930s, all shopping was done downtown and, during this busy season, all the stores and sidewalks were packed with excited people full of Christmas goodwill.

Always in search of the ideal gift, for the earnest shopper it was into a warm store then back out into the cold, and back into another warm store. This process continued until each shopper had purchased gifts for everyone on his Christmas list.

When Christmas day finally arrived, all the children awoke early (if they slept at all), quickly dressed in a cold bedroom, then made a mad dash into the living room to open their presents!

Under the brightly lit Christmas tree were the children's gifts of the 1930s, usually clothing items such as sweaters, sweat shirts (always gray), socks and pants. In addition to these expected necessities there might be a pair of skates, maybe a football or some type of game such as checkers or dominoes.

Even during the Depression, people acknowledged they still had much for which to be thankful. This was especially true at Christmas when all the community churches sponsored events which celebrated the spiritual aspect of the holiday season.

There were usually plays presenting the birth of Christ and the Christmas story was told repeatedly in Sunday school classes. From the church pulpits, the celebrated words about the birth of the Savior went forth to a weary and somewhat defeated people desperately seeking encouragement.

Although Christmas was a time of happiness for most, not everyone was able to share in its special magic. While everyone suffered during the Depression, for some unfortunates there was no Christmas tree, no presents and no Christmas dinner. For these children there was nothing, and their parents were left desperately trying to explain why Santa Claus did not stop at their house that year, even though others in the neighborhood received gifts.

Thankfully, for most young children of the 1930s, Christmas represented a special occasion: a joyous winter vacation, a time of gift giving and presents, and a time of being with friends and family.

Christmas was, and always will be, a celebration for children. Even the dark years of the 1930s could not dim the natural joys of this special holiday; oblivious to the hardships of the Depression, the wonderful thrill of the season survived in the hearts of the children of America.

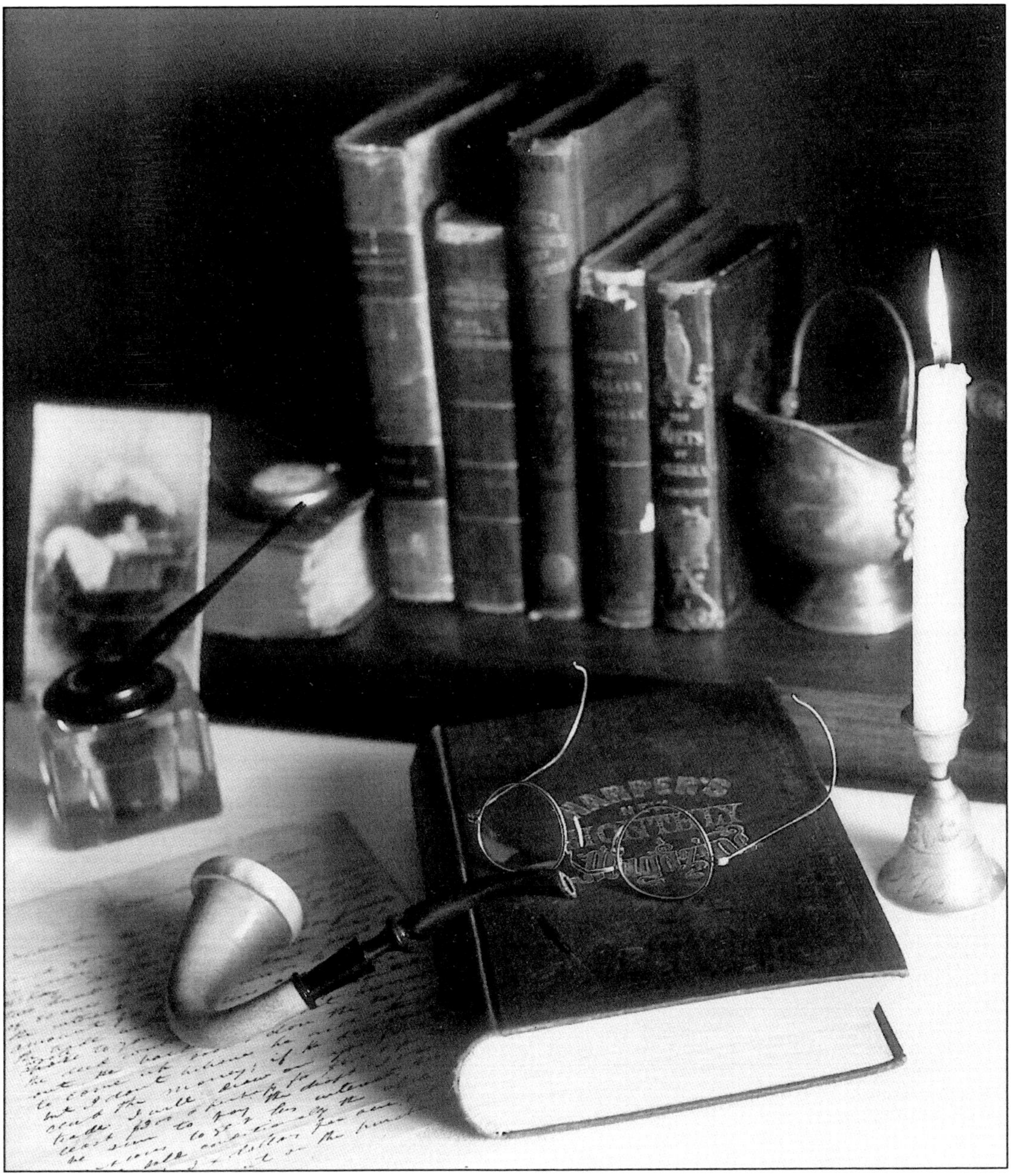

During the Depression, a family doctor would sometimes write off his bill because the patient was unable to pay.

A Doctor's Visit

If a person became sick during the 1930s, they seldom went to see the doctor at his office. Instead, the patient's family would call the doctor and he would make a house call.

The doctor would come to the house to make the diagnosis, although he was never called to a home unless the patient was seriously ill. Whatever the problem, the fee for a house call was rarely more than $2.

When a person was sick, sometimes the best that could be done was to administer a home remedy. Since almost every neighbor had an opinion on how to treat the illness, there was no shortage of home remedies. Whether they ever worked or not is another matter.

Another popular technique of that era was preventive medicine. It was somewhat akin to spring cleaning of the body. For people of that generation, preventive medicine usually meant one thing—a laxative, such as the notoriously distasteful castor oil, or a dose of sulphur and molasses.

For various reasons, it was rare during the 1930s for a person to visit the hospital. When a hospital stay was necessary, it was usually for either one of two reasons: surgery or broken bones.

Since most people were treated for their illness at home, most deaths occurred there as well. Following a death, and after the body had been prepared for burial, it was returned home. Here, it was constantly attended by friends and family members until the time of the funeral. In those days, all funerals were held at the church.

Like so much from that earlier era, the days when a doctor made house calls are left only to memory. In those years a family had a personal relationship with its doctor and viewed him not only as a physician, but as a friend. If a patient's family was short of cash the doctor understood and arrangements were made. In some cases, the bills were never settled and the pay for his services simply written off.

Although the medical profession has made tremendous strides since the 1930s, some things have been lost in the process. Sadly, the days of the old family physician, who was able to comfort his patients emotionally beyond their physical needs, seems to be a casualty of progress.

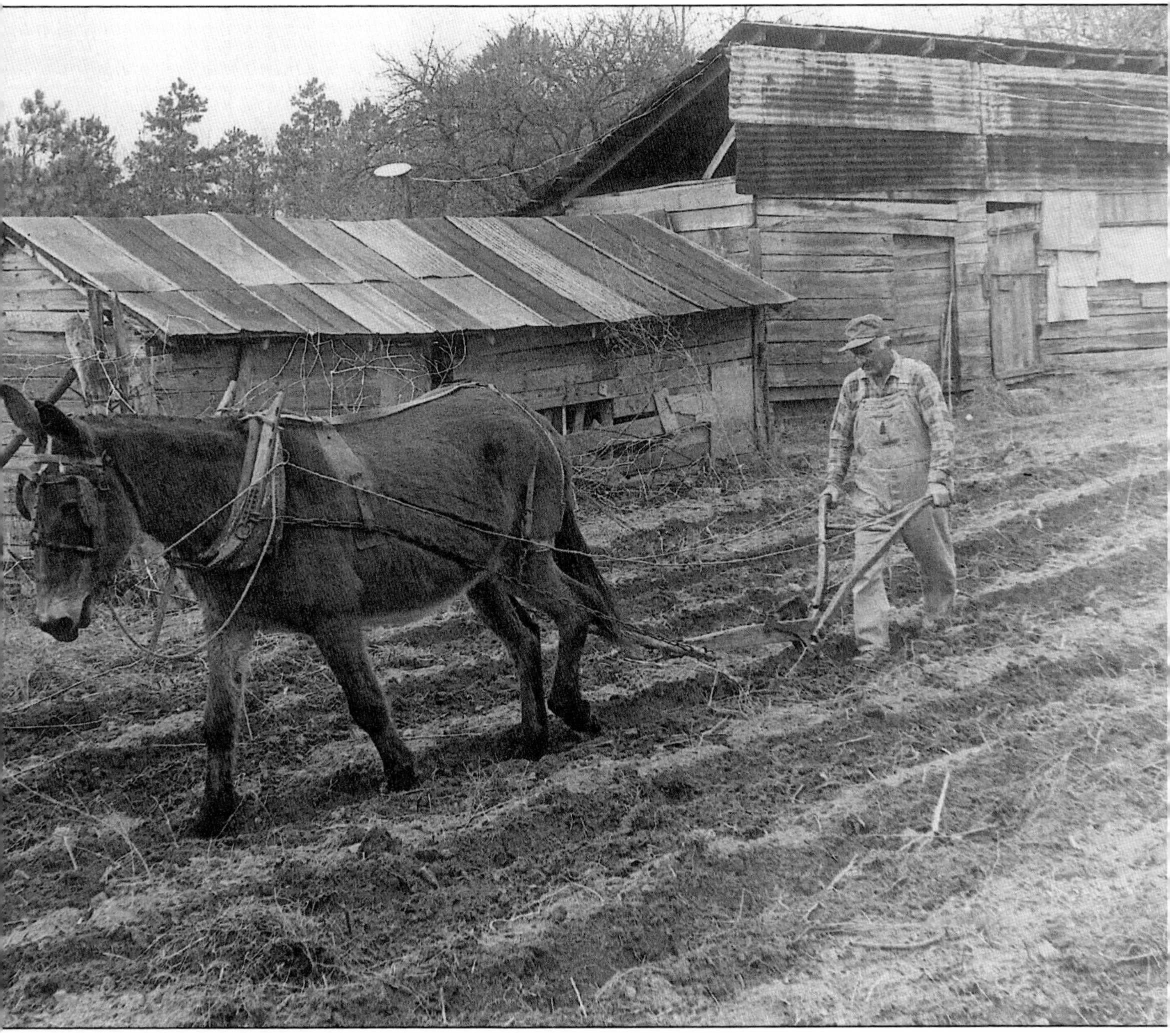

During the Depression, the only way to plow a garden was with a mule.

FAMILY GARDEN

After a long, cold, rainy winter everyone always looked forward to warm weather. The arrival of the first robin was not the ultimate harbinger of spring; for gardeners, the arrival of the first seed catalogue meant spring planting was close-at-hand.

During this time, each potential gardener would pour over his catalogue and, with great optimism, work up an order for seeds. In the mind's eye it was easy to visualize a perfect garden in full bloom, just as pictured in the colorful catalogue. Unfortunately, things rarely worked out that way and the vegetables would usually fall short of the pictures.

This shortcoming never deterred a disciplined gardener. Year after year, with the arrival of spring, he would take up a turning fork and prepare a small portion of the garden for early vegetables, such as lettuce, radishes, onions, and cabbage.

Later, if the family was not properly equipped, someone who owned a mule and plow would be hired to turn the rest of the garden. After the turning, the man would use a spike harrow to break up the clods and further smooth the ground.

When this step was completed, a push plow was used to lay out the rows. The final step was the actual planting, with most home gardens laid out in tomatoes, squash, cucumbers, okra, green beans, corn, and butter beans.

Depending on the weather conditions, it would take a garden a while to start producing. Once it did, the garden provided more than enough fresh vegetables for a family's use during the summer.

In those days, people would use everything their garden produced. Since a garden was planned to provide beyond a family's immediate needs, the extra vegetables would be canned for use during the coming winter. Favorite canning vegetables included tomatoes, green beans, and corn, or a soup stock made of tomatoes, okra, corn, and cabbage.

After all the work and planning, a family garden was a source of pride and enjoyment. While many good, economical meals came from a garden in season, during the cold winter months when fresh vegetables were scarce, the canned items represented a summer job well done.

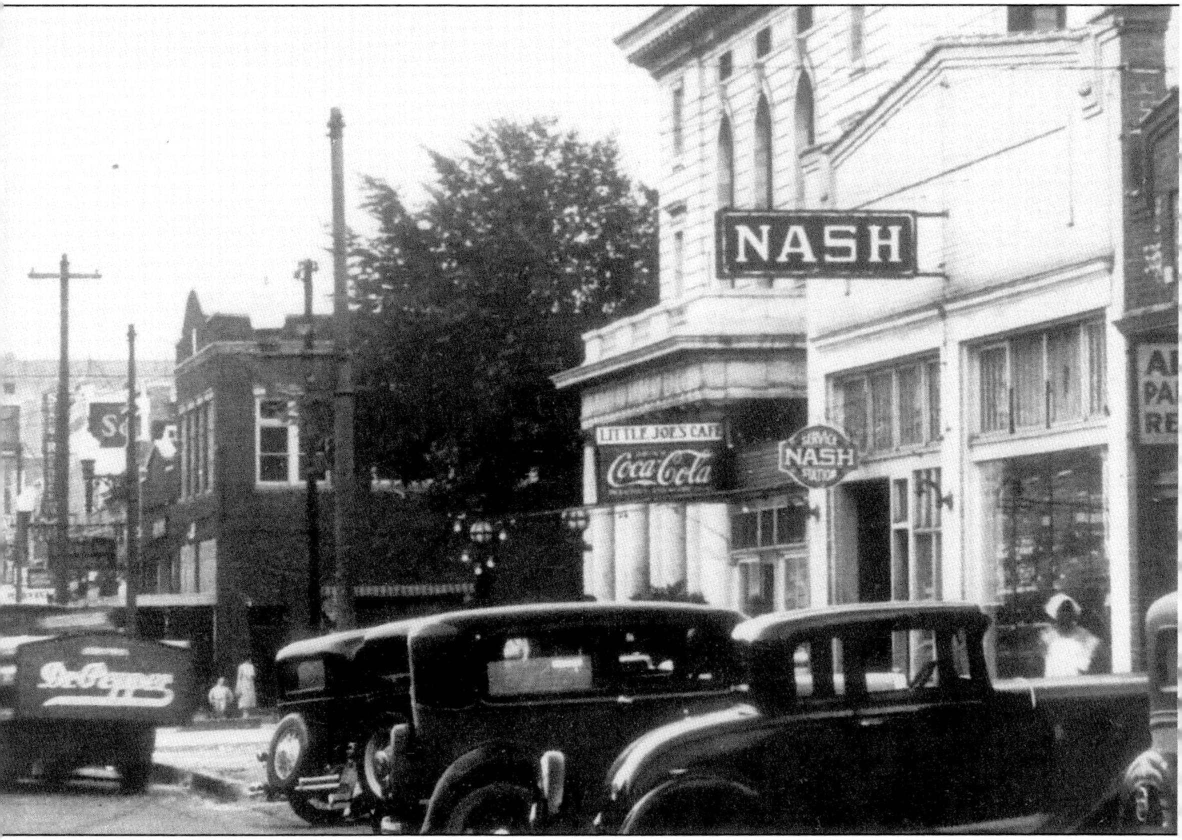

The Nash dealership, like others of that era, was located in the busy downtown district of Gadsden.

Our Cars

Even with an economy in turmoil, new cars came out regularly in the fall during the 1930s. Each dealer would announce when his vehicles would arrive and, for those interested, it was a chance to view the newest models. It was also a cheap form of entertainment for everyone, whether or not they had any intention of buying.

The center of commerce was the downtown district, so that's where the car dealerships were located. While every dealer had their own showroom, their stock usually included only three or four vehicles.

In the fall of 1929, when the new models were presented, my father's family purchased a 1930 green Chevrolet sedan, later affectionately named "The Green Turtle." It was a great improvement over their previous automobiles.

"The last T-model my parents bought was a coupe with just enough seating room for them. As a result, I had to ride lying down in a small space behind the seat," my father remembered.

The 1930 Chevrolet was the first car my grandfather drove with a gear shift. On the way home from the dealership the car stalled on the railroad tracks. Unable to restart the engine and with a train coming, my father's parents had to jump out and push it off the tracks!

"When I started driving in 1935, I learned in that car," my father said. "The first skill I mastered was how to keep the vehicle moving and not stall the engine."

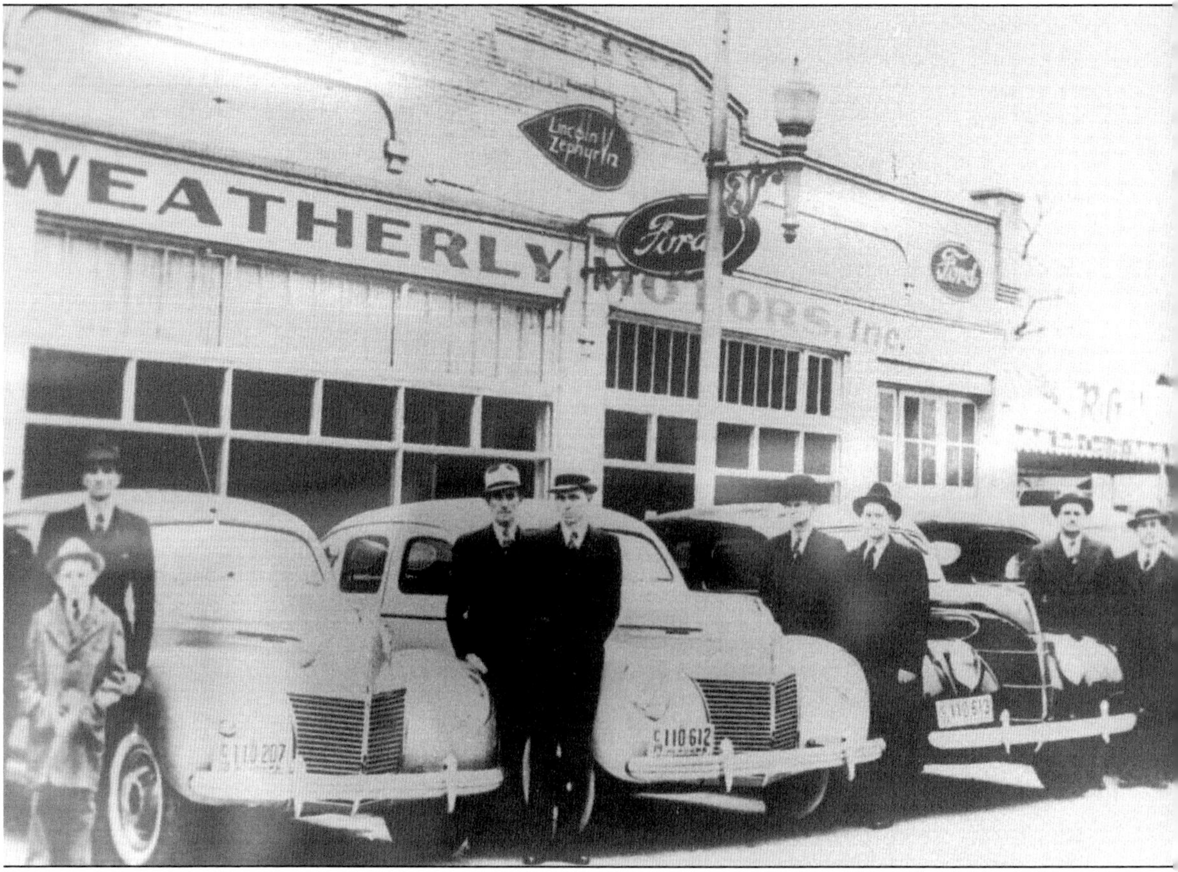

The Ford dealership on Broad Street displays its new model cars in 1939.

In 1936, "The Green Turtle" was traded for a new Chevrolet. Unlike today, at that time General Motors only produced two models of Chevrolets: a "Standard" and a "Deluxe." The major difference in these makes was that the "Deluxe" featured a radio and "knee-action" front wheels (which provided for a smoother ride), while the "Standard" had no extras.

At one time this car was loaned to a family member (an uncle) who wrecked it. Although it was repaired, the job never suited my grandfather, who traded it in for a Lafayette in 1938.

The Lafayette, a larger car than the Chevrolet, was manufactured by the Nash Company.

"This is the car I drove when I first started dating my wife," my father remembers. "She may have married me thinking my family had money, since I drove a big car. To her amusement, she later found out all the money my family had was invested in the Lafayette!"

While the vehicles of the 1930s were not designed solely as pleasure vehicles, one of the big improvements in construction included more seating room, radios, and heaters. Even with these new additions, air-conditioning was still unheard of.

When the decade of the 1930s began, all cars looked like a box. Improvements were quickly made however, and by the decade's close the cars became more aerodynamic and attractive to the customer. Regardless of their specific appearance, all these vehicles were a big leap from the horse and buggy days of just a few generations before.

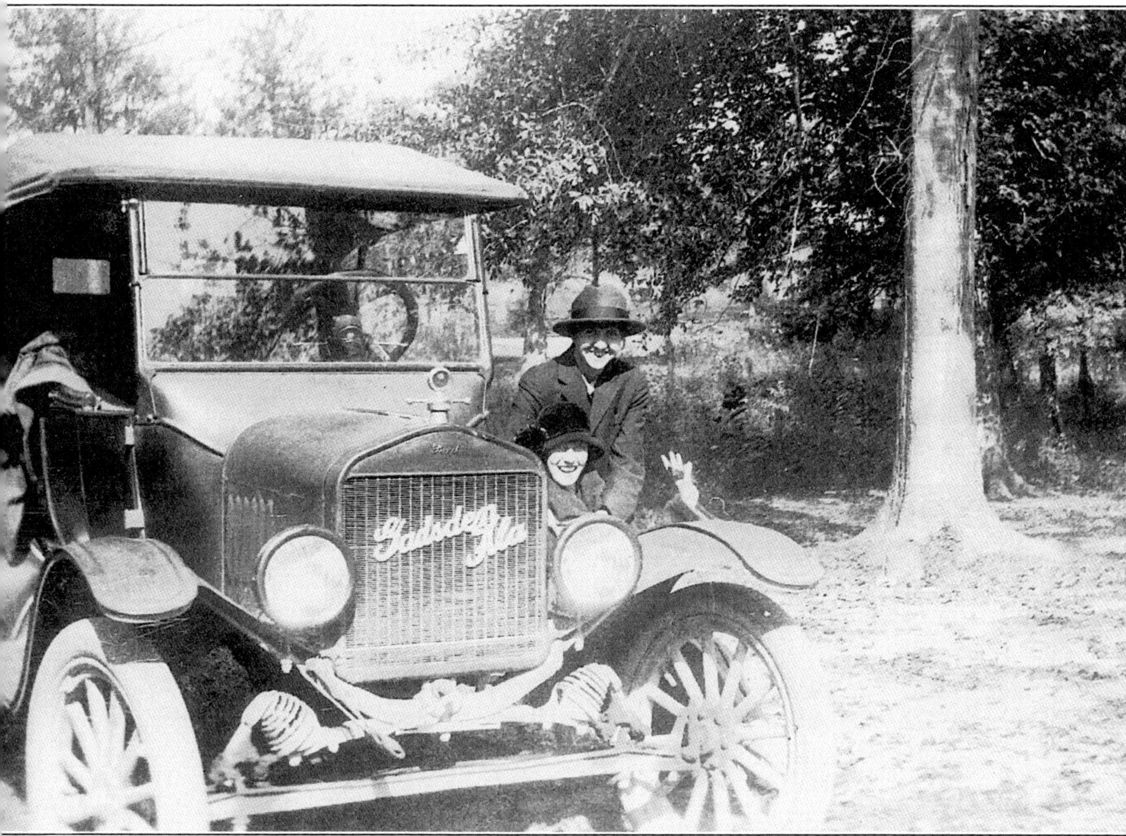

A proud motorist displays the words "Gadsden, ALA" on his radiator for everyone to see.

AUTOMOBILES

The automobile was both a luxury and a status symbol during the Depression. Buying an automobile then was an unusual experience, something special.

With a limited number of prospective customers, competition was extremely keen. Once the dealers discovered a person was actually considering making a purchase, their salesmen would come to the house each driving a new car and offer a test ride. In this manner, competing salesmen would attempt to persuade each person to try out *their* particular make of car.

The purchase of an automobile turned into an event for the entire neighborhood. When someone finally bought a car and brought it home, all the neighbors would be interested in the new vehicle.

There were many makes of automobile during these years. Besides the vehicles produced by the Big Three (namely General Motors, Ford, and Chrysler), there were many smaller companies manufacturing cars. Essex, Whippet, Hudson, Terraplane, Chandler, Studebaker, Nash, and Packard were a few of these.

Back then, cars were not used frivolously. An automobile was primarily used as transportation to and from work, for important business, or necessary errands around town. Due to the hard times, very few vacations or unnecessary trips were made as the result of a shortage of money to buy gas.

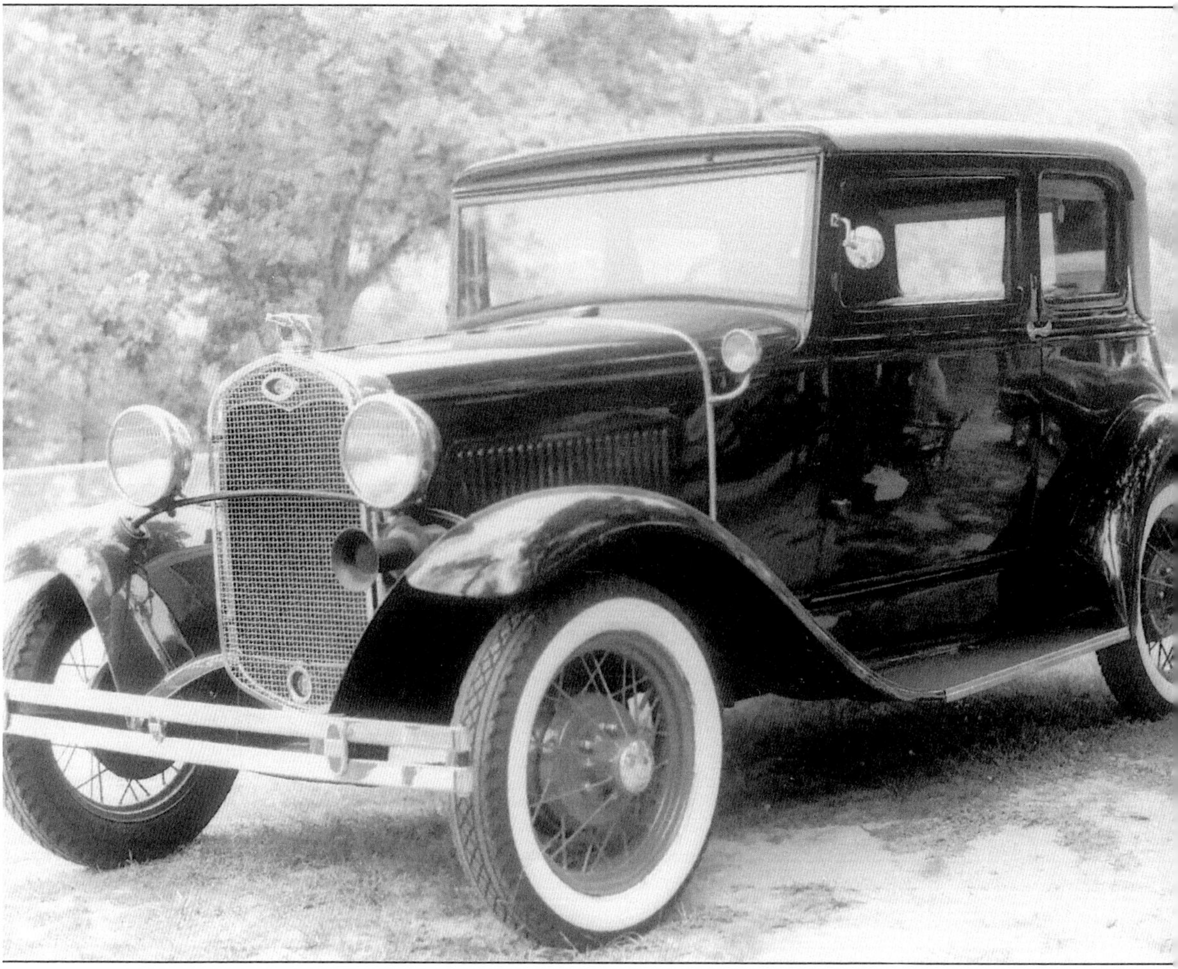

Shown here is a 1930 model Ford.

The condition of the roads was another reason why people didn't travel widely. During the 1930s, there were many primary roads still unpaved, and many country roads were practically impassable during the harsh winter months.

Traveling on these primitive roads was often eventful. The best technique was to simply put the car in the ruts, hold on, and try to stay there. If a driver met another car and was forced out of the ruts, inevitably the vehicle ended up in a ditch.

With his car stuck in the mud, the driver would have to rely on a team of mules for help.

Even if a driver was lucky enough to escape this fate, there was always the danger of dragging the oil pan, losing all the oil, and burning up the car's engine.

During these days of eventful road trips, obstacles came in every form. Sometimes when two vehicles met at a narrow spot, one or the other would have to back up to a place where it was wide enough for them to pass.

When the weather turned hot in the summer, the best way to cool off would be to take an evening ride. Another enjoyable experience was to drive downtown on Saturday night, park, and simply watch people doing their shopping. In those days, the stores remained open until nine p.m.

The train depot was one more destination which provided enjoyment and diversion

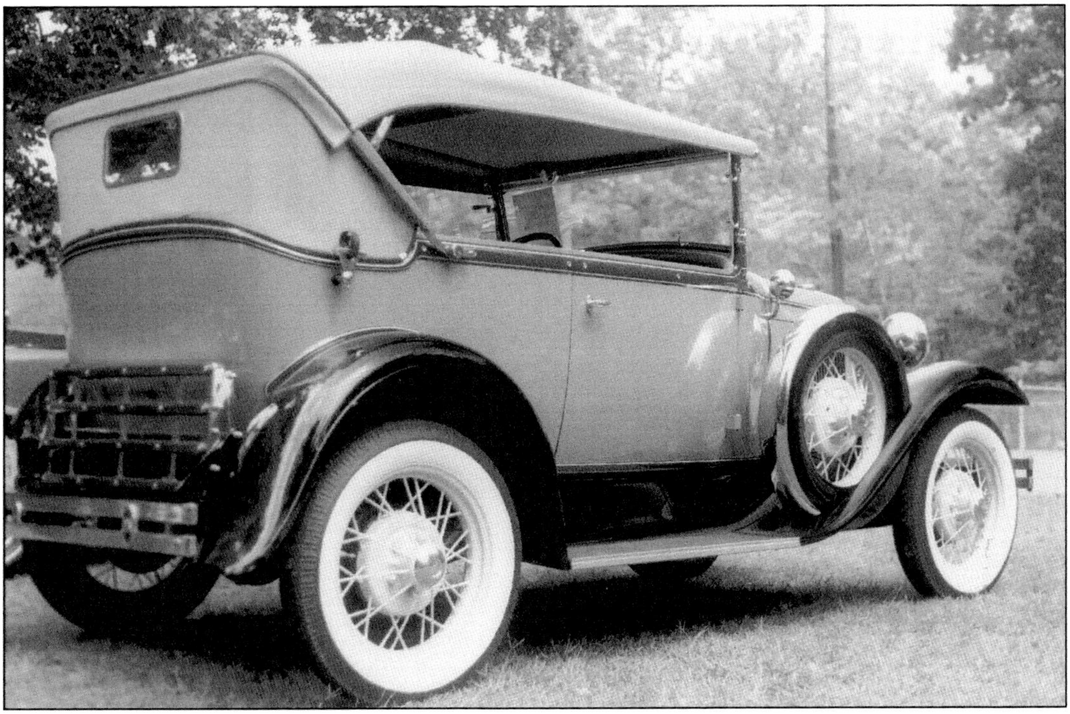

Above is a 1930 Ford sedan touring car.

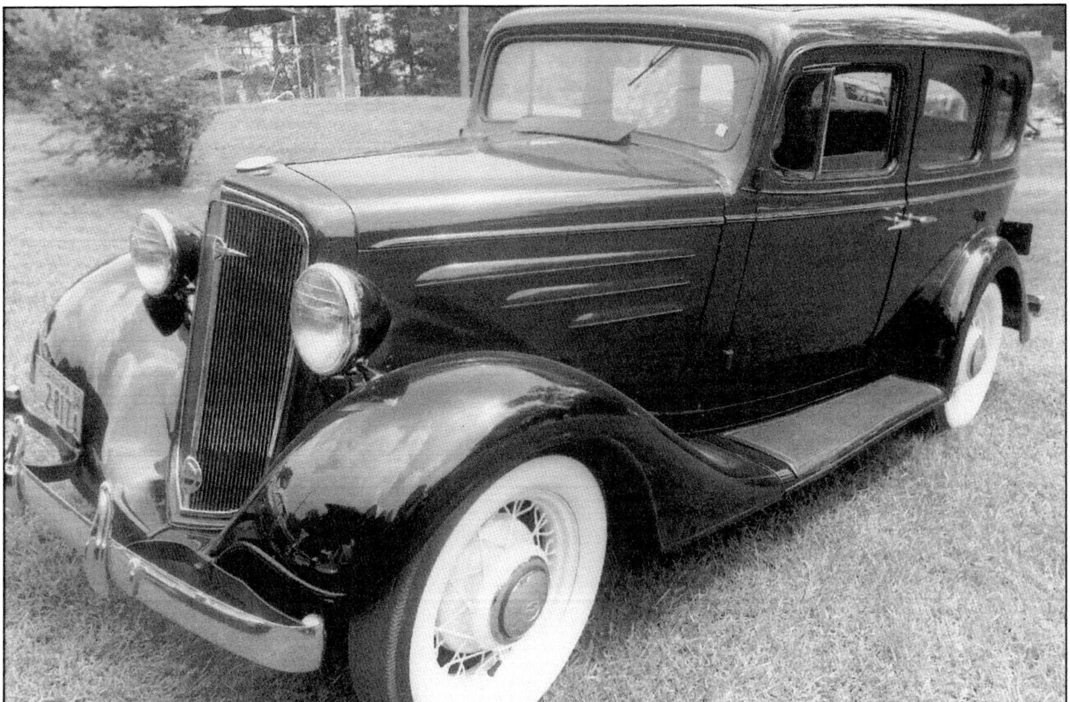

This is a 1934 Chevrolet.

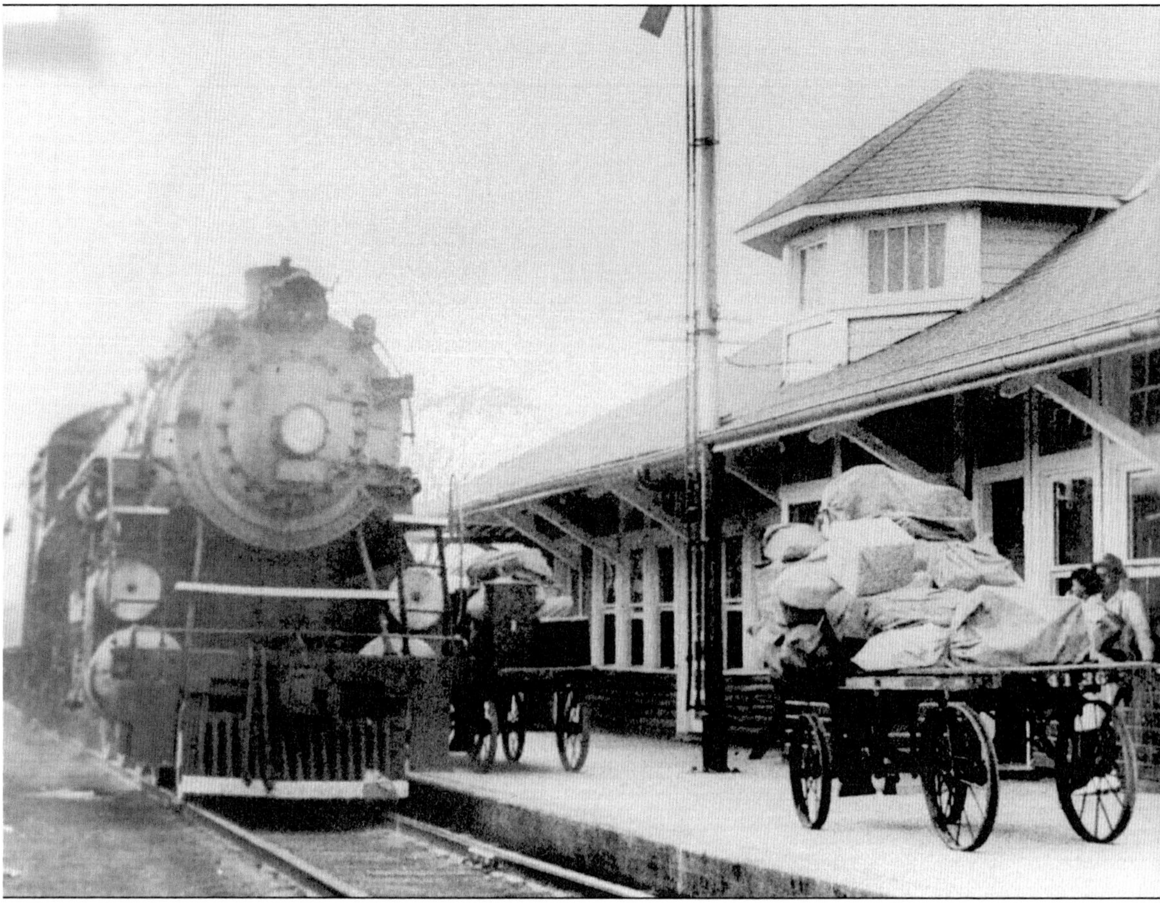

The appearance of a train provided enjoyment and diversion during the Depression.

during the Depression. People would drive their cars to the depot just to watch the arrival or departure of trains.

Since times were hard, the appearance of a train started everyone to dreaming as to where those fortunate enough to travel were going, or where they came from? What kind of life were they escaping from, or heading toward?

Because times were difficult and money tight, most people could not afford the cost of a train ticket, let alone the extravagance of owning an automobile. It took everything they earned to exist day-to-day.

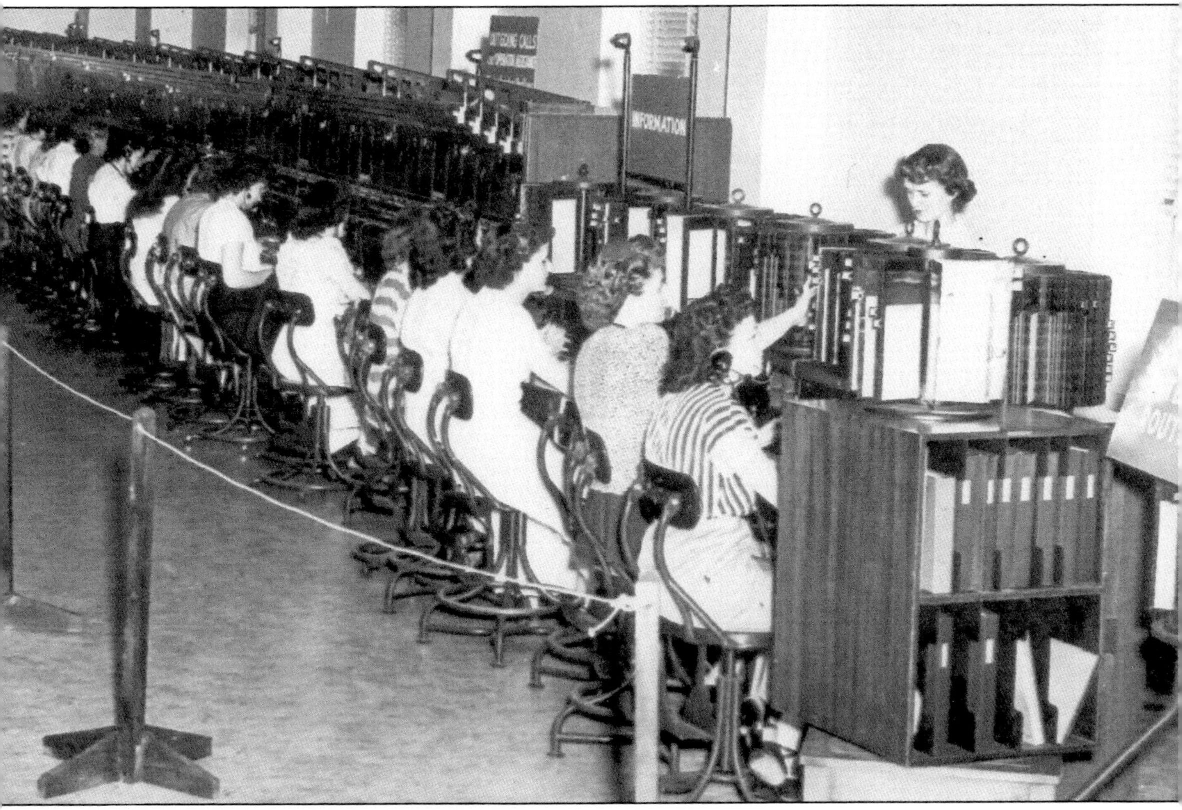

Women operated the telephone switchboard.

TELEPHONES

During the hard years of the Depression, a telephone was a luxury only a small number of people could afford. Fortunately, or unfortunately, my father's family was one of the select few in their neighborhood to own a phone. As it turned out, the phone became more of a "public property" than just a family possession.

Friendliness was a hallmark of those years—a time when neighbors helped each other whenever possible. Sometimes this custom had strange repercussions. An example of this is when a neighbor came to visit, all the time really wanting to use the phone.

When they reached the front door, the person would simply say: "I've come to use the phone." Then they'd walk right into the house, as if it were their own home.

A troublesome part of this arrangement was when someone would call and want to speak to a neighbor. As a child, it was my father's duty to go to their house and tell them they were wanted on *his* phone.

The telephones of that era sat upright, with a black, bell-shaped receiver on a hook. To use the phone, the caller would pick up the receiver, then wait for the operator to say: "Number, please."

The caller would give the operator the number he was trying to reach and she would plug it into that exchange on her switchboard. In the early years of the phone system, the operators were always women.

At this time, each phone was either a private, a two-party, or a four-party line. It was especially difficult to use the phone if a family was on a party line because someone else might have it in operation. Many times

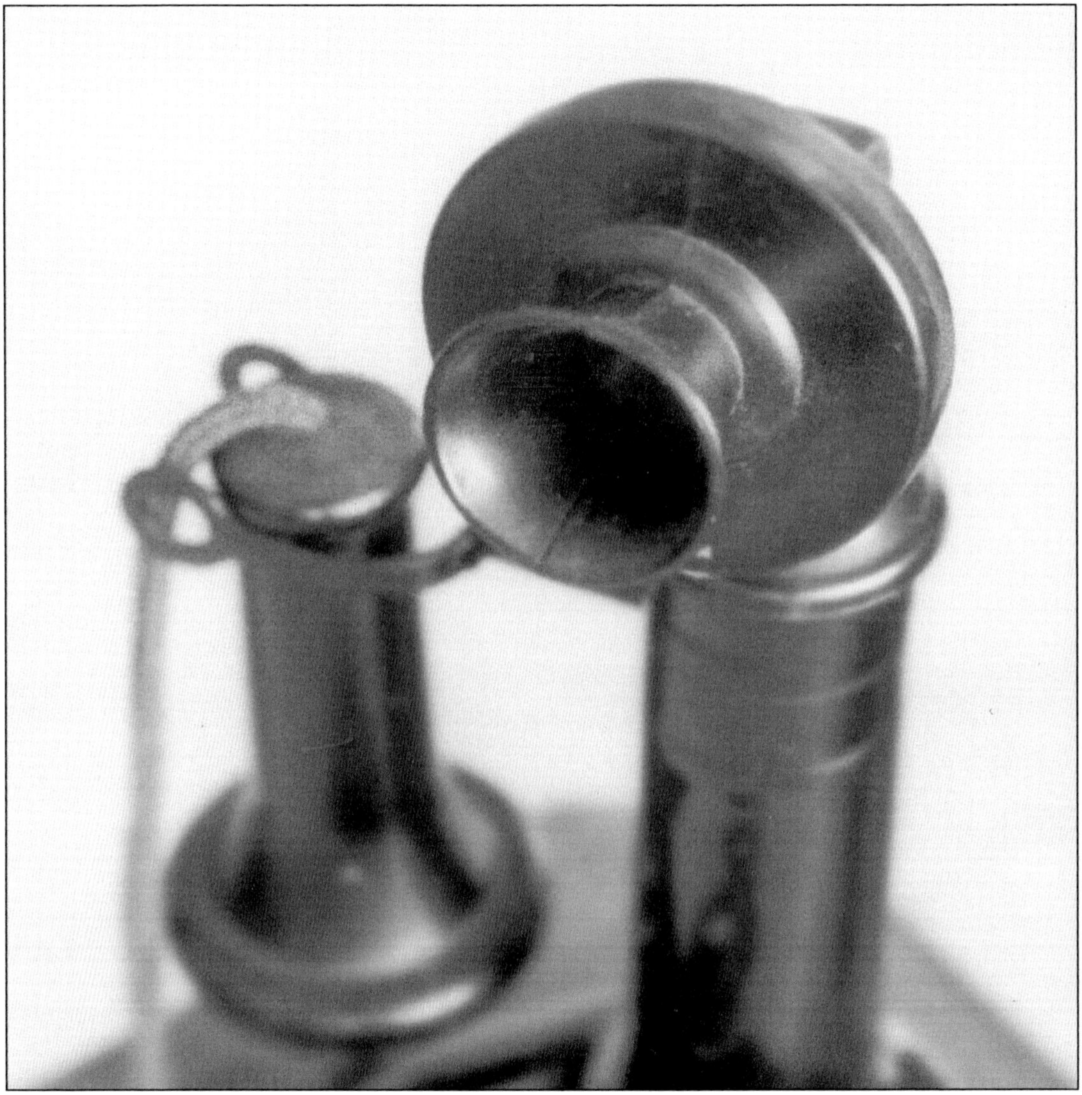

"Number, please?" During the Depression, my father's phone number was 434-J.

a person picked up the receiver to hear a conversation already in progress.

How many rumors were started because of nosy people listening in on party line conversation?

To minimize confusion on a party line arrangement, each customer was assigned a specific ring. For example, one of the parties might be given one ring, while another might identify themselves with two rings. If the phone rang twice in your house—and your family had the one-ring code—it was an indication that the call was for someone else.

After all these years, one thing I find amazing is my father remembers his telephone number: 434-J. He says it is as clear to him now as the actual ring of that old telephone.

As you look back on the development of the phone system in America, it is hard to believe such a simple instrument as a telephone would be considered a luxury. My, how the times have changed!

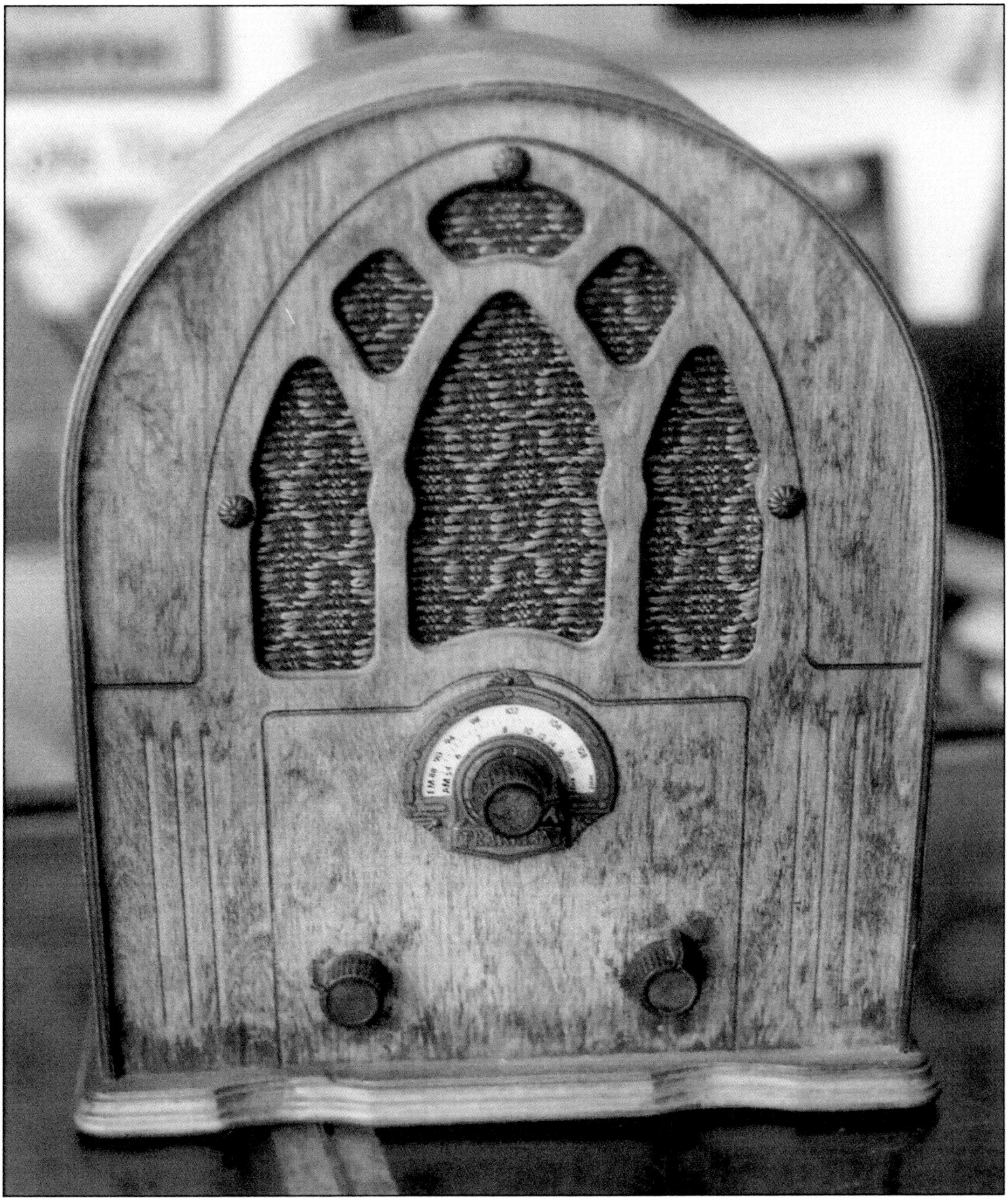

During the Depression, families gathered around the radio to listen to their favorite programs, such as "Amos 'n' Andy" and "Lum and Abner."

RADIO

The medium of radio came into its own during the 1930s. It proved to be a great benefit for the suffering nation because people had no money, and radio furnished a cheap form of amusement.

The programs of the day consisted of musicals, comedies, dramas and mysteries. There was never any concern

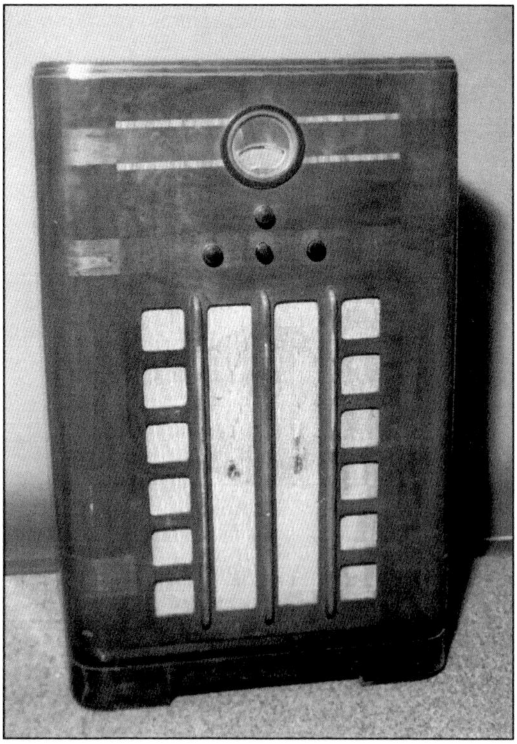

Seen here is a floor style radio of the Depression era. In the 1930s, radio programs were welcomed into the home like a friend.

over questionable content, because all presentations were wholesome and acceptable to the entire family.

Some of the most popular shows of that era were the musicals, with big bands such as Guy Lombardo, Benny Goodman, Tommy Dorsey, Jimmy Dorsey and Harry James. The comedians who kept people laughing during the Depression included Jack Benny, Fred Allen, Ed Wynn, and Eddie Cantor. Perhaps the best recognized mystery program was "The Shadow."

Two of the best known daytime programs were "Amos 'n' Andy" and "Lum and Abner." Both of these shows came on late in the afternoon and since there was not much activity in the neighborhood, practically everyone listened to these broadcasts.

It was said during the summer when all the windows were open, a person could walk down the street and hear the same program coming out of every house. Not even a line of dialogue would be missed!

With the radio medium in its infancy, the type of reception depended on the style of aerial. A common type used by many houses came in under the eve, extended the length of the building, with a lead-in wire through the window attached to the radio.

A second type of aerial was a homemade device with a wire extended between two boards nailed at opposite ends of the house, above the roof. From this set-up, a lead-in wire fed into the room.

Regardless of the kind of aerial, reception could easily be affected by the weather. High temperatures, rain, or thunderstorms all caused frequent problems resulting in whistling or static. Late at night, a weak signal could easily be overrun by a more powerful station.

Still, with all of these technical problems, it was possible to turn a radio dial and pick up stations from as far away as New Orleans, Pittsburgh, Cincinnati or Chicago—where a person could listen in on another world beyond their own.

During the Depression, when people were deprived of so much, a radio provided great entertainment. For every family who owned one, the radio was a welcomed addition to the household.

With such an extreme shortage of money, the radio supplied the cheapest diversion from the harsh realities of the day. All of these old radio programs were invited into Depression-era homes as cherished friends.

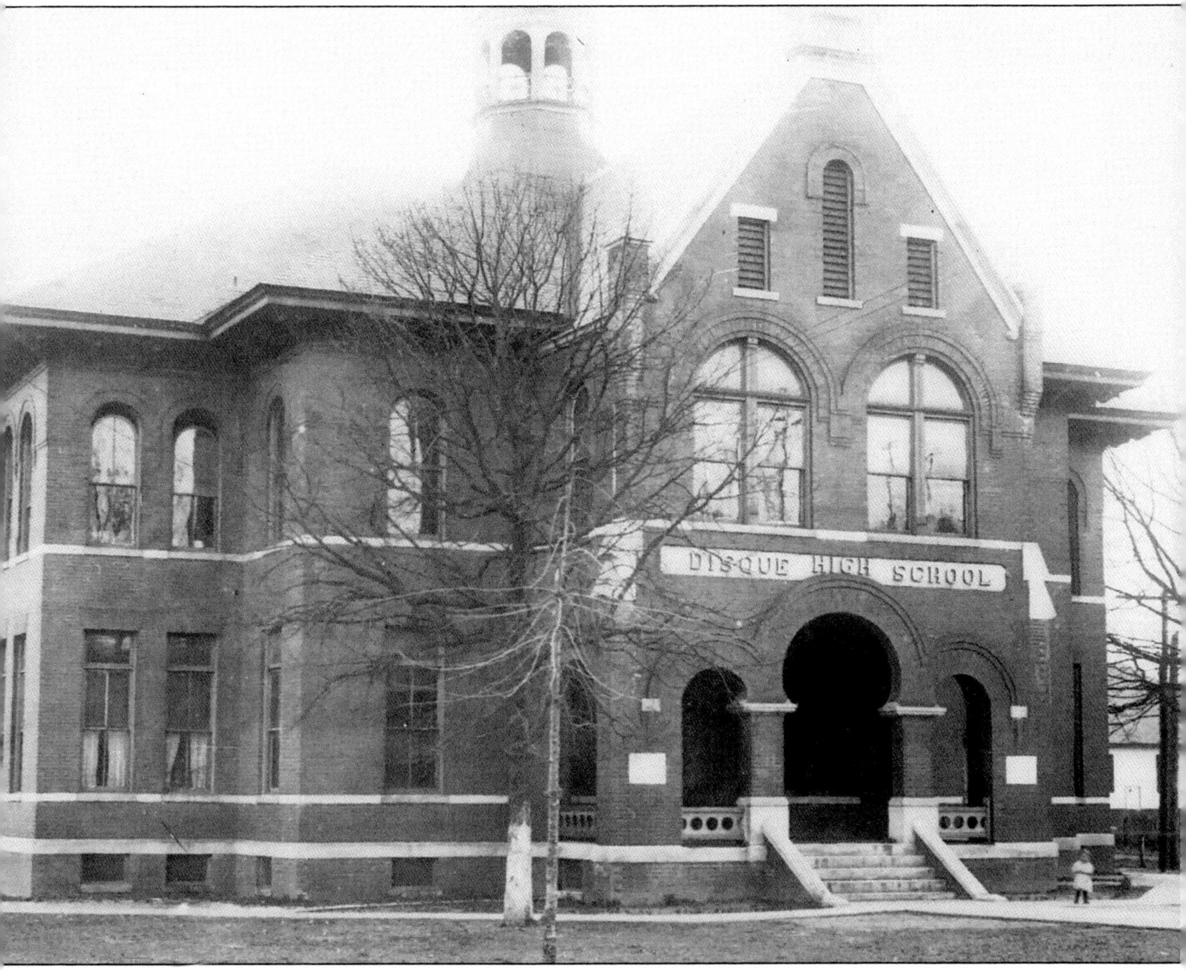

This image of Disque High School was taken before it became a junior high school.

Schools

Practically all students walked to school during the Depression. Since schools were centrally located in the neighborhood this did not present a problem, except when the weather was extremely cold or raining.

Before school started in September, it was important for every student to purchase the necessary clothing for the coming year. A raincoat was essential because, regardless of how hard it was raining, each student left home in time to reach school before the late bell rang.

An aviator's cap (made famous by Charles Lindburg) was another necessity for the boys. On cold mornings something was needed to cover up young ears. Even with a raincoat and an aviator's cap, many days a student arrived both wet and cold.

During this time, practically all students brought their lunch from home in a brown paper bag. Although the schools had lunchrooms, only a few students purchased a lunch because sandwiches were the main item sold—the same food they could bring from home.

Most rainy days it was difficult for a student to arrive at school with a lunch that was not either wet or smashed, because it had to be carried under an arm to keep it dry.

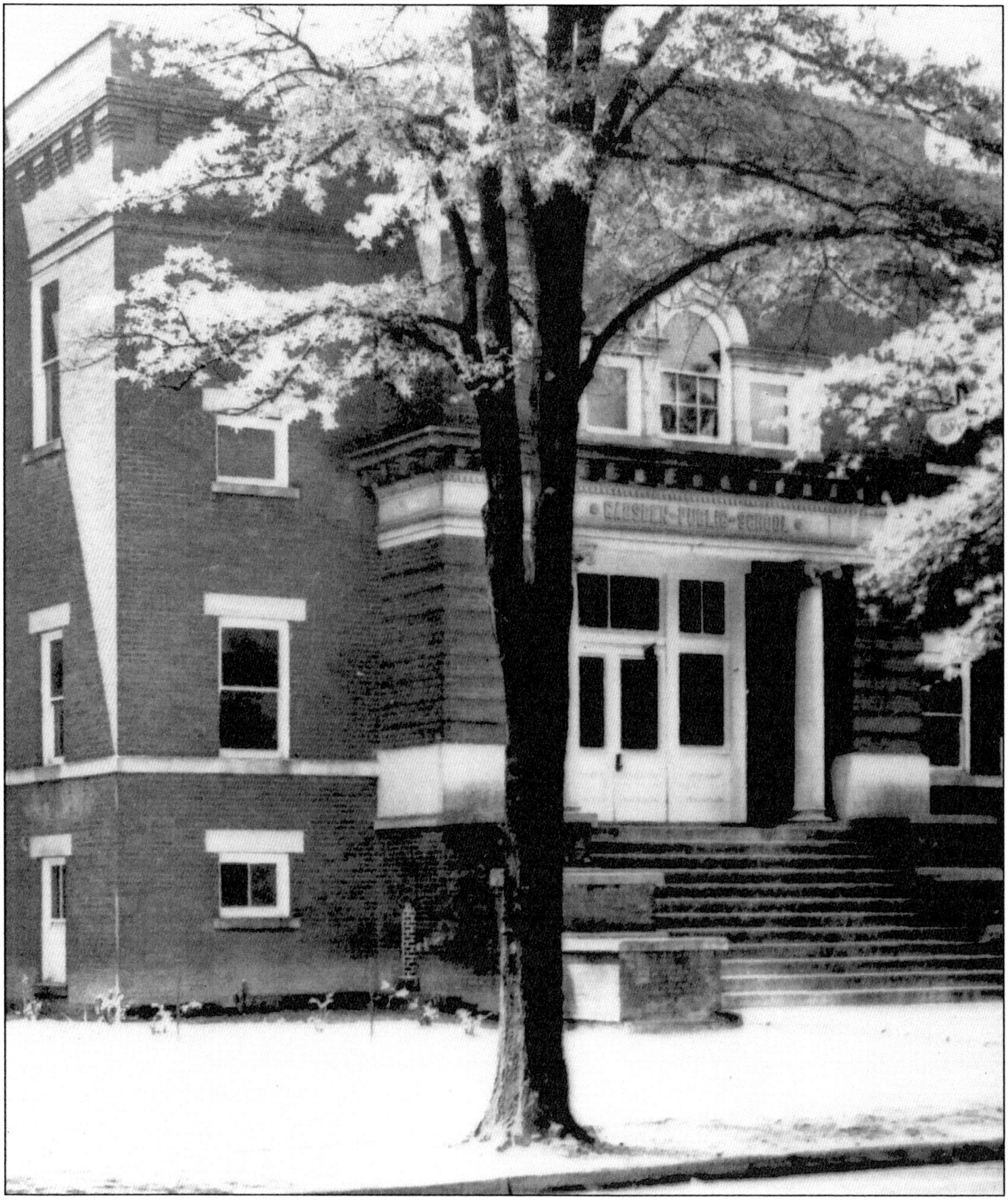

My father started his school days at the Eleventh Street School.

Many of the school teachers from that era were very instrumental in molding a young person's character. Not only were they educators but, in those days, a school teacher was one of the most respected people in the community. One of the reasons for this is because they were some of the best educated people of that day. All of them had college educations at a time when just a small number of people in the community had even a high school diploma.

The schools were places of discipline. The teachers demanded—and got—complete

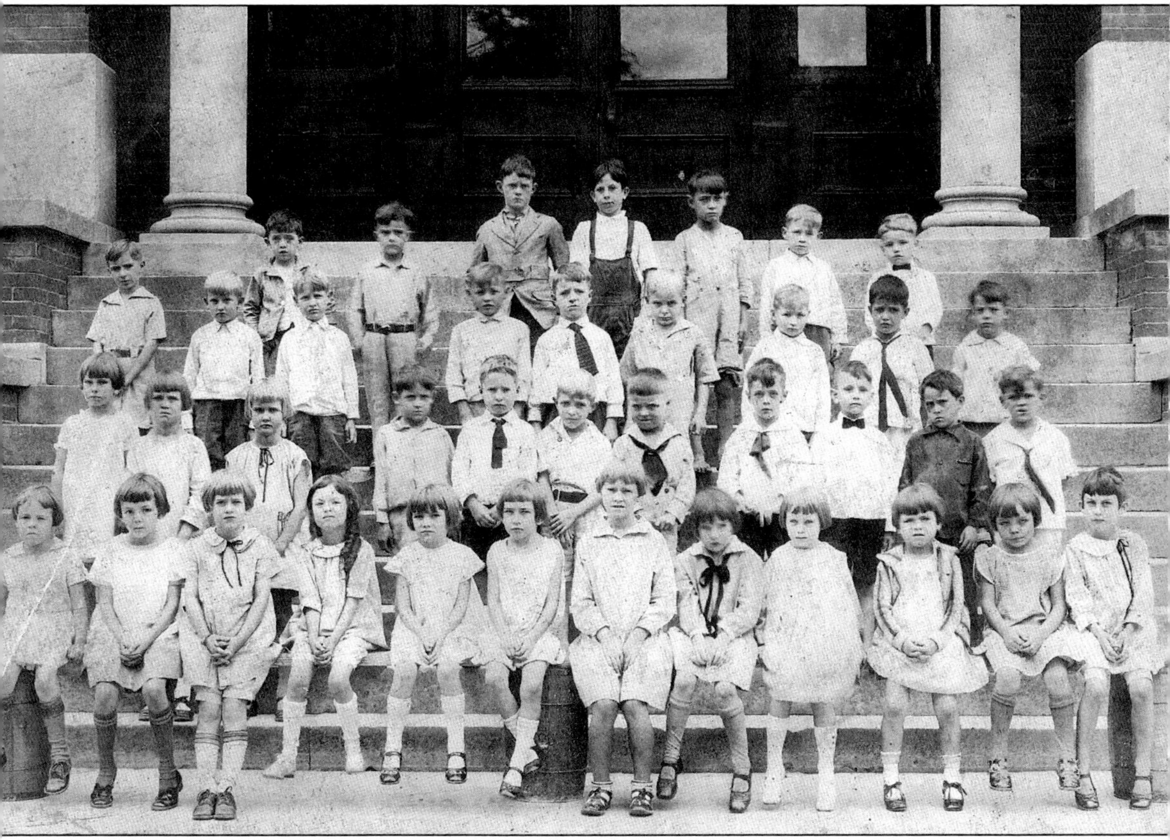

These children attended the Eleventh Street School in Gadsden. My father is in the second row, the third from the right.

respect. If a student found himself in trouble at school, it was certain he would also be in trouble at home!

While most students probably enjoyed their school days, they always looked forward to the holidays: Thanksgiving and Christmas. But more than these days off, all students eagerly anticipated the three-month summer vacation.

Even though students enjoyed their summer holidays, during the hard times of the Depression it was rare for a family to leave home on a vacation. Although my father grew up in a Southern state that bordered Florida, he never saw the "Sunshine State" until he was stationed there by Uncle Sam during World War II.

Today, with all the difficulties in our public institutions, the schools of the Depression era seemed in some ways better equipped to prepare children for the future. With no advanced technology, they taught discipline and demanded respect and, in the process, formed character in their young students.

Snow Days

In the Deep South, it was a rare occasion when there was enough snow and the temperature was cold enough for it to stick. If it did, though, snow always created some great excitement for the kids.

The biggest reason for jubilation was that snow forced schools to close. Mothers didn't look at it the same way as children, however. What was a great joy for them

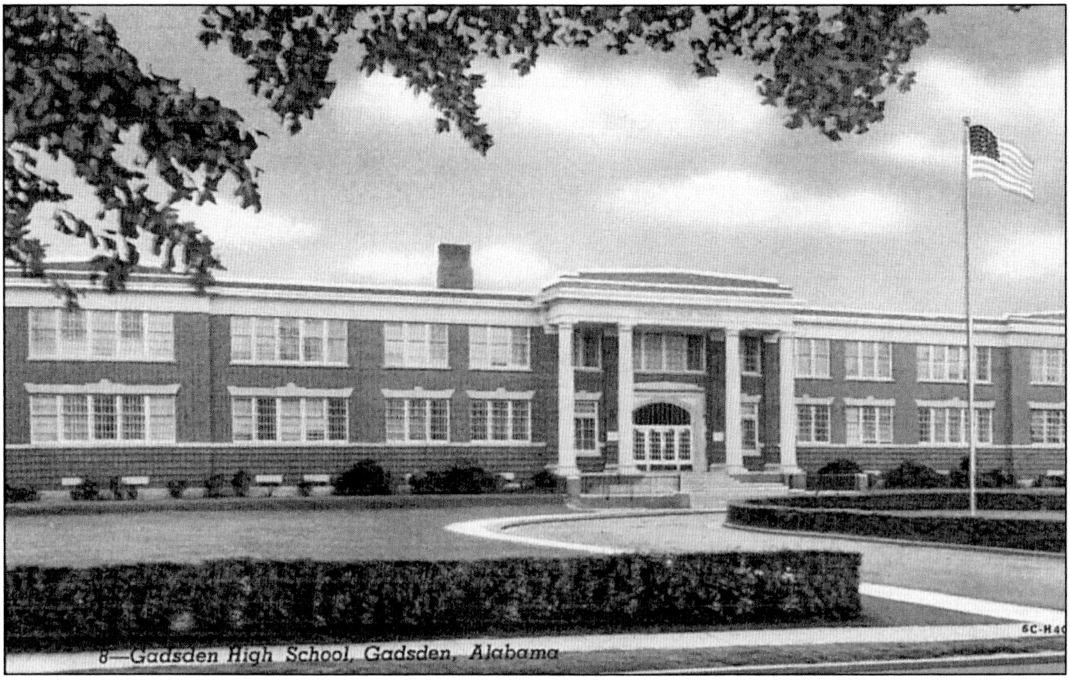

This postcard of Gadsden High School was produced in the 1930s.

became just extra work for their mothers.

For mothers who could never keep their excited children from playing in the snow, it meant constant changing and drying of wet clothes.

Before dryers became commonplace, the only way to dry clothes in the winter was to hang them in front of the fireplace or heater. While the children were playing outside, the inside of the house was cluttered with chairs in front of the fireplace, draped with wet clothes.

A snowy day in the South created challenges for young boys who were eager to make up for lost experiences. A sled was one of the first things they tried to build, and it was made from two, 2x4's for runners and several crosspieces to lie on. A rope would be attached on each side for support and to help pull it back up the hill.

A major problem with a homemade sled was that it was too heavy to operate and could not be steered. Not to be denied such fun, often a piece of cardboard, linoleum or a wash pan was substituted for a sled.

A hill was necessary for sledding and it was usually in a pasture. With snow covering everything, sometimes there were some messy and embarrassing wrecks.

Can you guess what natural obstacles were hit in a snow-covered cow pasture?

For Southerners, snow days were a rare and magical time. Living in a warmer climate, no one knew if it might be years before they were allowed such fun again. While the sledders might not have been well equipped, it's doubtful that anyone ever received more enjoyment than Southerners playing in the snow.

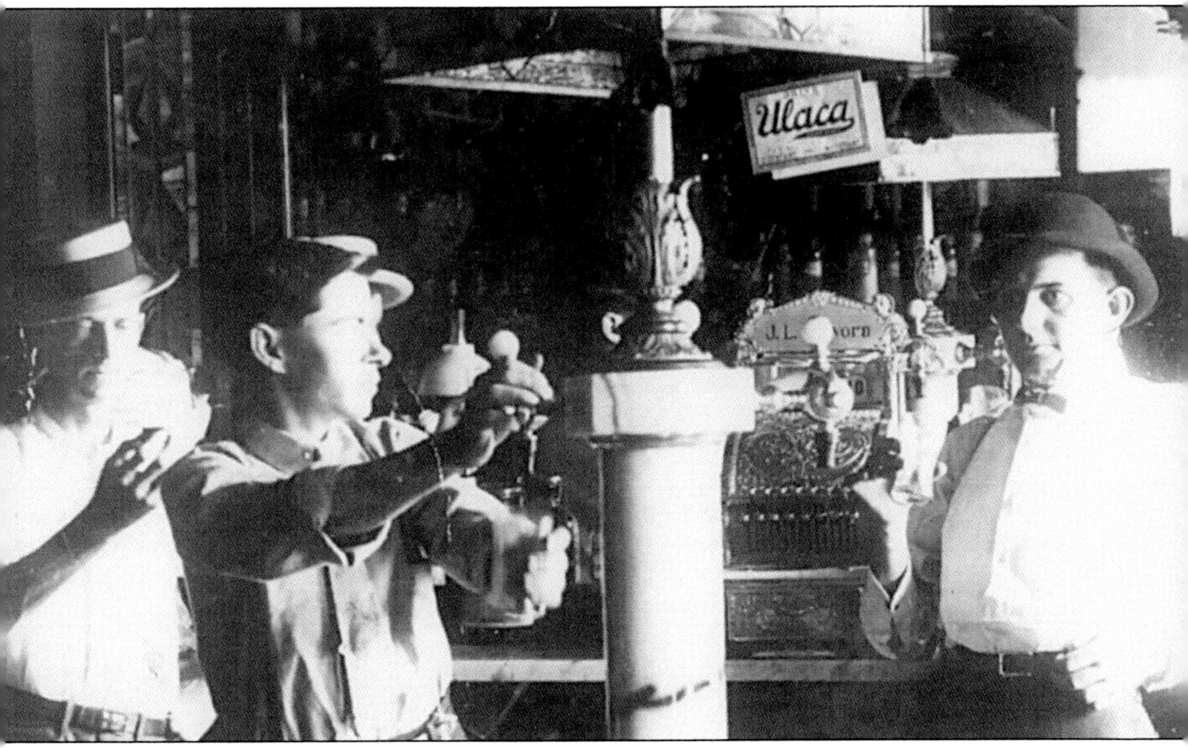

A special attraction at the drugstore was the soda fountain and boys "hoppin' curb." During the Depression, both men and young boys were eager to find work.

GETTING A JOB

Since all families were suffering during the Depression, extra income was always appreciated. In 1933, while my father was a freshman in high school, he decided to get a job.

"There was a man in our church whom I approached about a job. He managed a shoe store and hired me to work every day after school, and all day Saturday," my father said. "In return, he paid me the enormous salary of 75 cents a week."

When my father received his first payday he was surprised by his salary; it was $1, instead of the agreed-upon price of 75 cents. His happiness was short-lived though, because on his way home from work that night he somehow lost his money. For the first week of his working career he wound up netting zero!

Initially, my father's duties at the shoe store were janitorial work, washing windows and running the stock (keeping a complete supply of shoes on the shelves at all times).

He had not been employed too long when the manager permitted him to start selling shoes in the men's department. The most popular shoes at the time were Jarman, which produced the "Friendly Five" and the "Fortune." They sold for $5 and $4 per pair, respectively.

"With my change to sales I went on commission and my pay increased. Nor will I ever forget what happened the first Easter week I sold shoes," my father said. "Easter was the biggest selling period of the year and my commission for that one week was over twelve dollars."

But the store owner didn't want to pay him that amount of money. Presumably, he thought $12 was just too much to pay a 14-year-old boy.

To my father's good fortune, the owner relented and paid him the full amount, since the rate of commission had already been agreed upon.

"You can rest assured I was extremely proud of that payday, for never in my life had I ever possessed so much money."

All through high school, my father worked in the afternoon and on Saturday in some store. For promotion, one of these stores had a "bank night" every Saturday evening with a prize of $50. The people in the town could register by dropping their name in a tumbler, from which the winner would be drawn.

The store would be packed full of people awaiting the announcement of the winner's name, which was the idea behind the gimmick. With living conditions so hard, a $50 windfall was an enormous amount of money.

After graduating from high school in 1937, my father ended his retail sales career and went to work at the steel plant.

"I hired in as a common laborer for 28 cents an hour," he said, "and after a short time the minimum wage was raised to 32 cents an hour."

During this time, his job was bundling rods; later on, he went to work in the rod mill and the pay was based on tonnage. With this new job, the pay increased dramatically.

"In 1939 I left the steel plant and entered college, and I'm not really sure why. I don't know if it was ambition or whether it was because I was single and my work schedule ran from three until eleven p.m."

Either way, the end of the 1930s found my father in college.

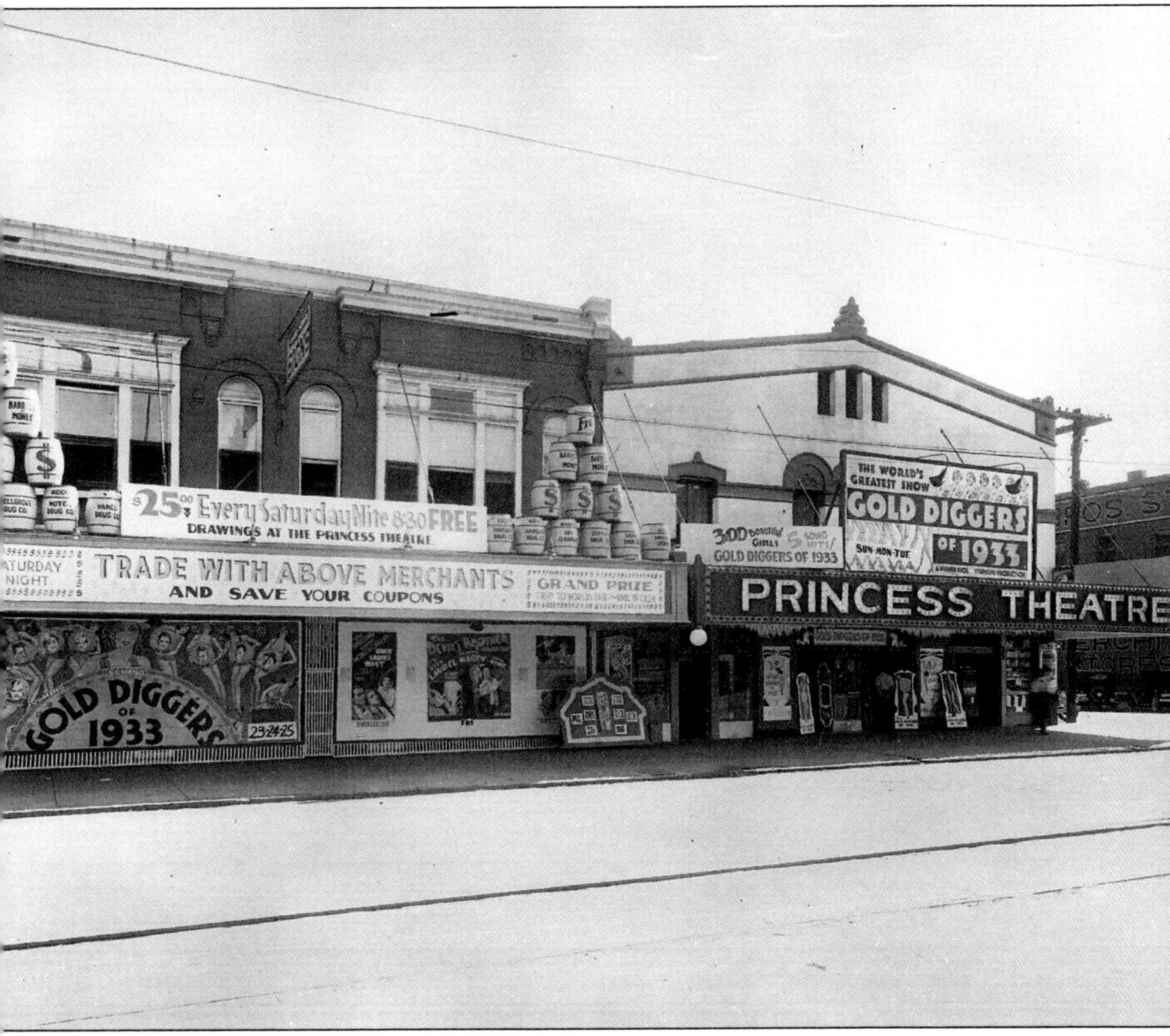

The Princess Theatre, on Broad Street in Gadsden, was a world of illusion far removed from the realities of the Depression.

ENTERTAINMENT

The Picture Show

The "movies," or "picture shows" as they were more commonly called during the '30s, were the most popular form of entertainment. Since the movies were a world of illusion, they became a great diversion from the hardships of the Depression. In this private, dimly lit world, a person became engrossed in the action of the screen and, for the moment, forgot all their problems.

While every attraction provided some form of escape, this was especially true of musicals such as the Golddigger Series and the Fred Astair and Ginger Rogers productions. These films, featuring lavish costumes and sets, were almost beyond the imagination of the ordinary citizen suffering through daily, austere living conditions.

Every Saturday, the theatres would feature a cowboy picture. In addition

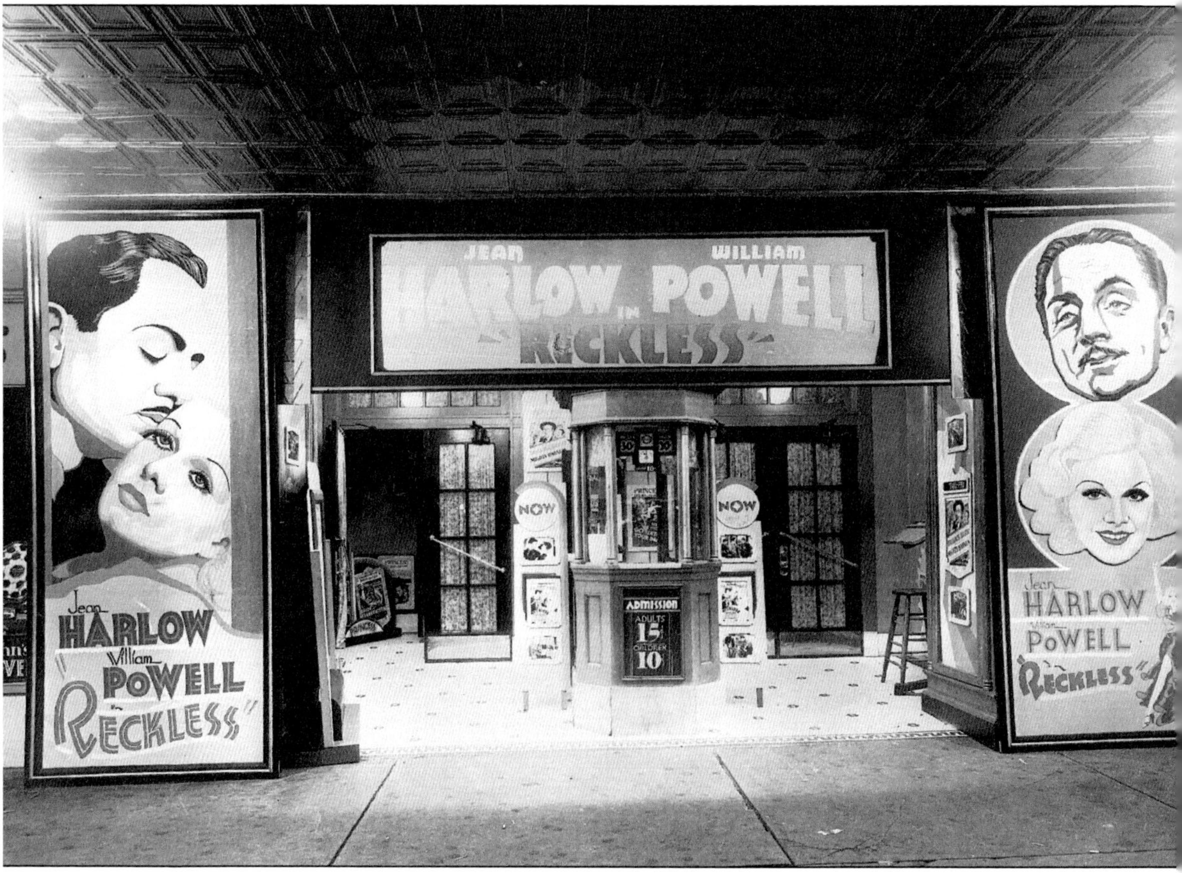

These advertisements show popular stars of the 1930s.

to this, there would be a comedy and a continued piece, which would run for weeks. Each segment would end with an exciting or suspenseful situation that would ensure, if at all possible, that the patron would return for the next week's installment.

"The Mysterious Rider," a western, and "The Last of the Mohicans," with Chingachgook and Magua as the last of a dying breed of Indians, were two famous continued pieces. Both of these were especially popular with young boys eager for excitement.

During the 1930s, many cowboys rode across the silver screen and found favor with their young audience. Cowboy actors Tom Mix, Buck Jones, Ken Maynard, Bob Steele, Tim McCoy, and Johnny Mack Brown were well-known to the '30s generation of movie goers.

Even though westerns and musicals were always in demand, two films made during that era attained instant cinematic immortality when they were first released. "The Wizard of Oz" and "Gone With The Wind," both filmed in 1939, are still pleasing audiences to this day.

"When 'Gone With The Wind' was released I was in college and came home one weekend to attend a showing," my father remembered. "My dad purchased two reserved seats for us at the unheard-of price of one dollar each. It was the only time I know that our local theatre ever reserved seats."

When these shows appeared the normal price of a theatre ticket rose from 15 to

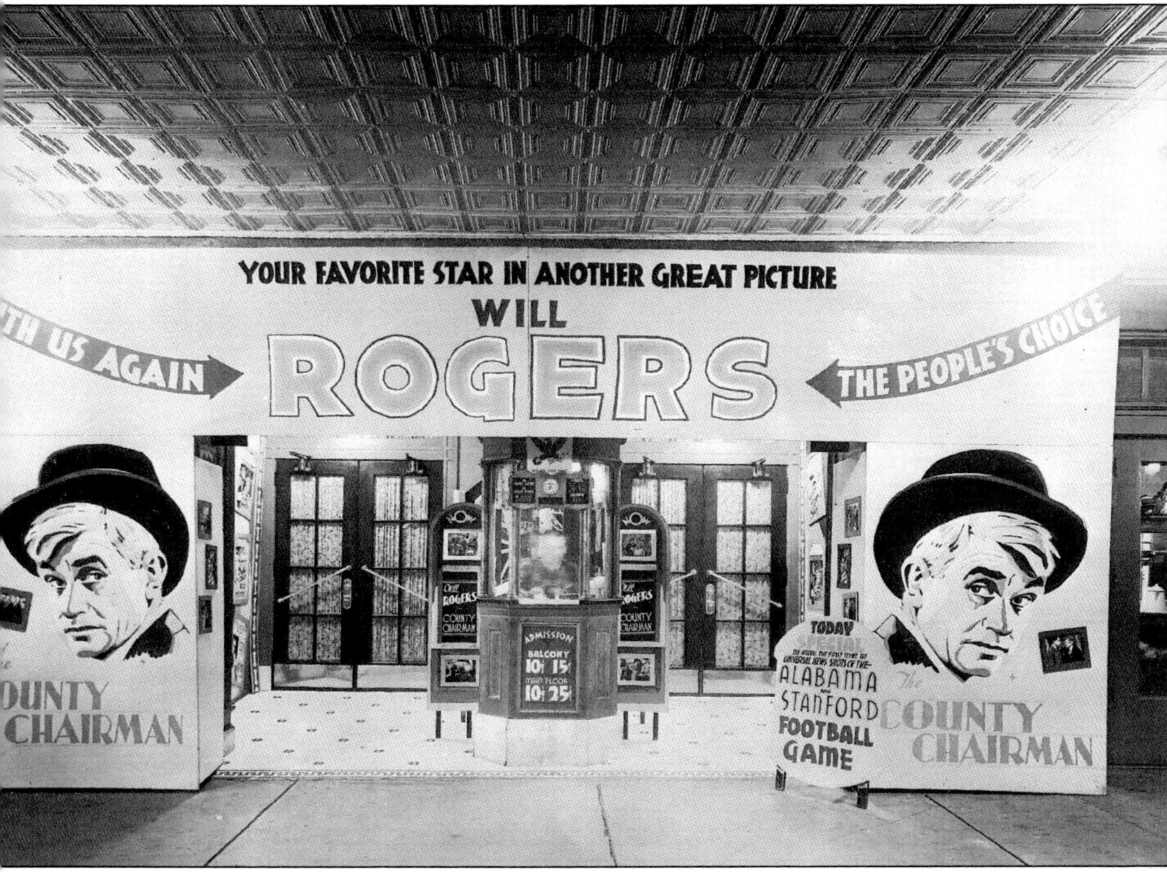

A poster of Will Rogers beckons customers into the Princess Theatre. Notice the 15 cent admission fee.

25 cents. However, at mid-week some theatres would sponsor a "nickel day," which permitted a patron to view a movie and a vaudeville for 5 cents.

Once these young customers grew up, the main activity for dating couples was to attend a movie. After the show the couple would go for a milkshake and a hamburger; this was considered a big event and it all would cost less than a dollar bill!

During the hard days of the Great Depression, a visit into the dark arena of the theatre was a trip into a magical world of illusion, far removed from the harsh realities of everyday life. With such promotional techniques as continued pieces and comedies, the theatres kept their customers returning week after week to a world of make-believe that only Hollywood and the motion pictures could provide.

Circus

The circus was a big event during the 1930s and was eagerly awaited by both children and adults.

When my father was young, the circus always came to town in the spring and fall. In the spring, the circus troupe would move out of its winter quarters in Florida and work its way toward the northern states. After a season up North, in the fall it would reverse its course and return to Florida.

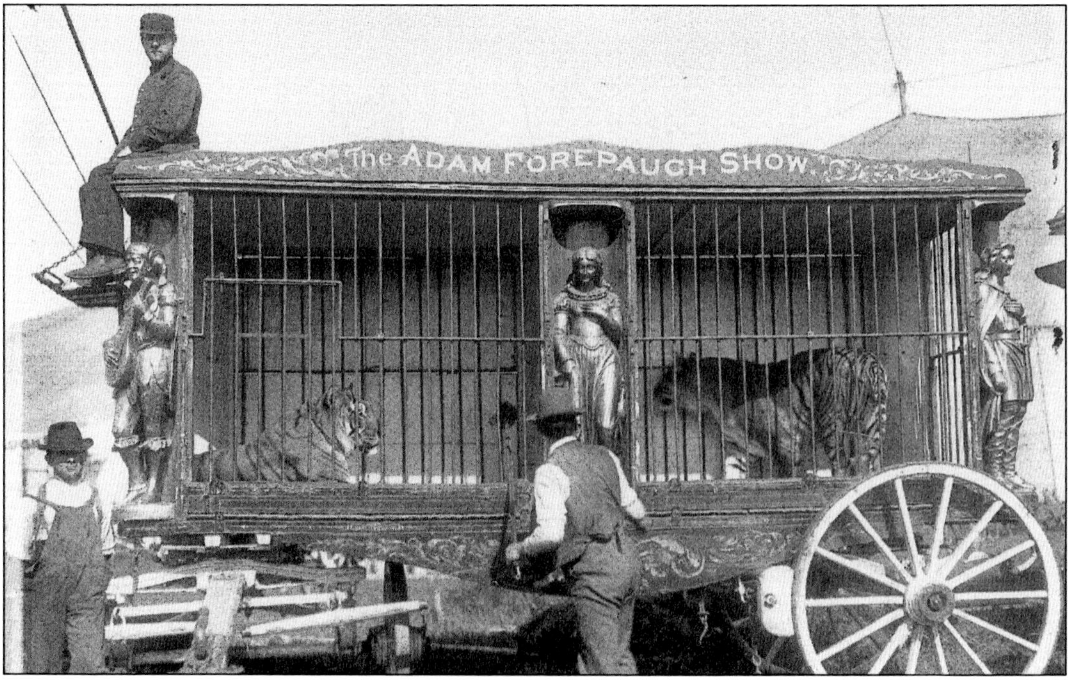

A circus wagon with live animals always attracted a crowd.

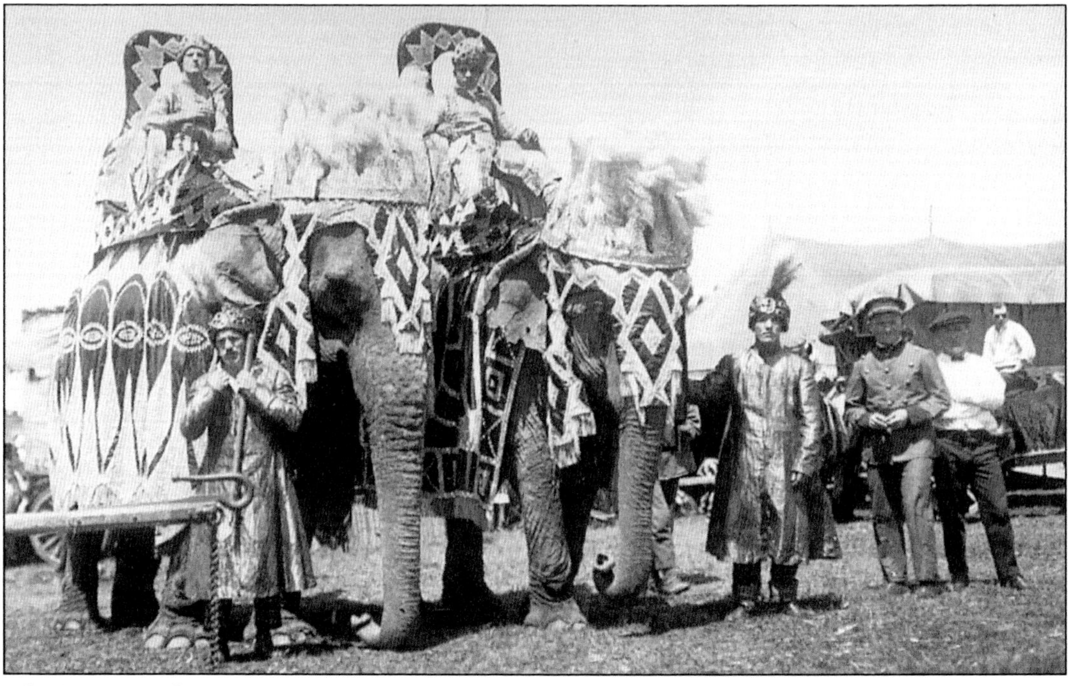

Elephants and entertainers were usually featured in a circus parade.

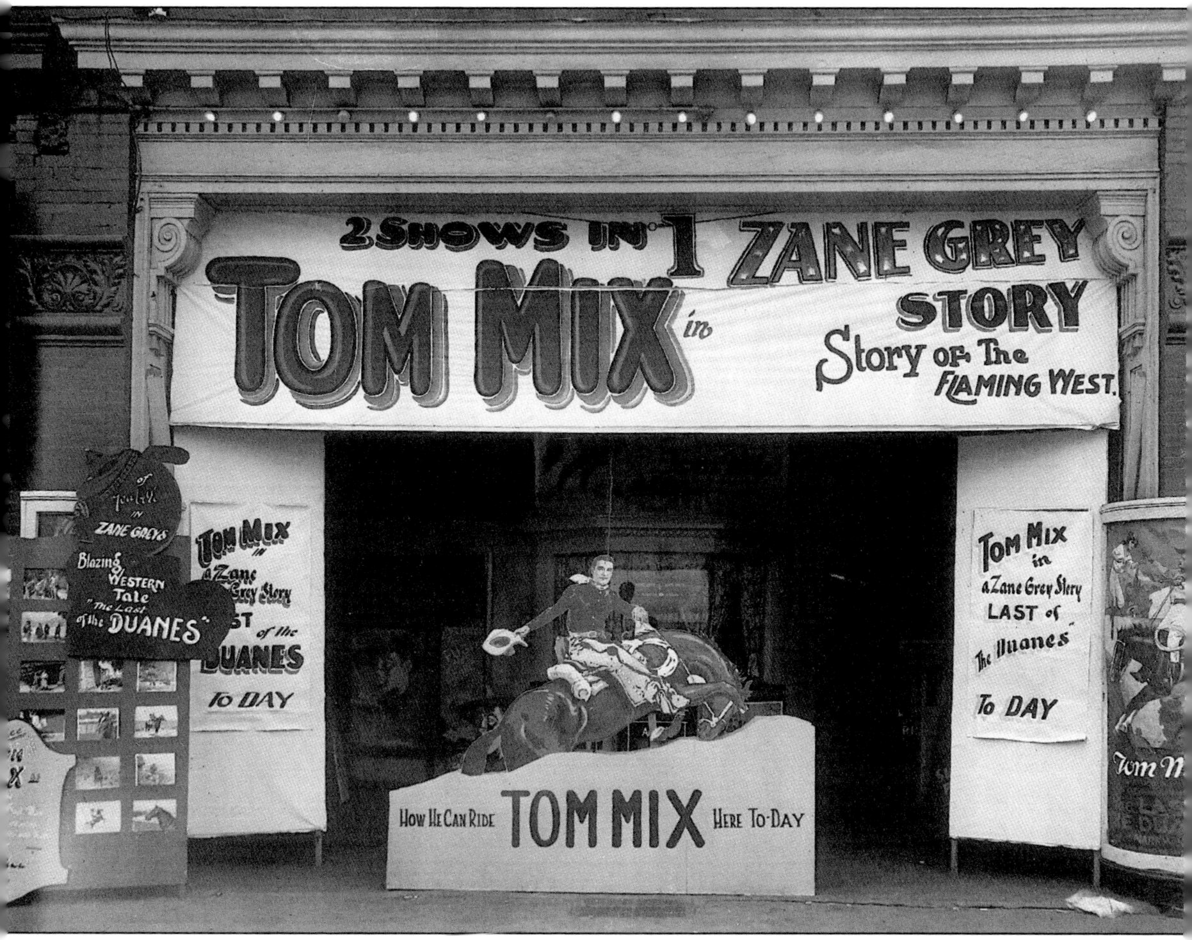

My father went to see Tom Mix at the circus and ate so much cotton candy that he became sick.

To build up anticipation, the first sign of a circus coming to town was the advertisements placed on windows of vacant stores. On the day of the performance, the circus train would arrive and anyone could go to the railroad spur to watch it being unloaded.

Before anything else was removed, the circus wagons that held live animals were taken off the flat cars. Then the horses would be hitched to the wagons, to pull them to the site where the circus was scheduled to encamp.

"Even if a person could not afford a ticket to the main event, at least it was possible to see the animals for free when they were being unloaded," my father said.

Although the circus world might appear glamorous to youngsters, and some young minds dreamed about joining, it was not an easy life to follow. To keep the show on the road required a contribution from each circus member.

The roust-a-bouts, who were responsible for much of the daily, behind-the-scenes work, were kept constantly busy and seldom slept, except during the performances.

As a self-contained world, even animals traveling with the circus troupe played their part. In this environment the elephants, especially, provided more than just entertainment. They played a major role in setting up "The Greatest Show on

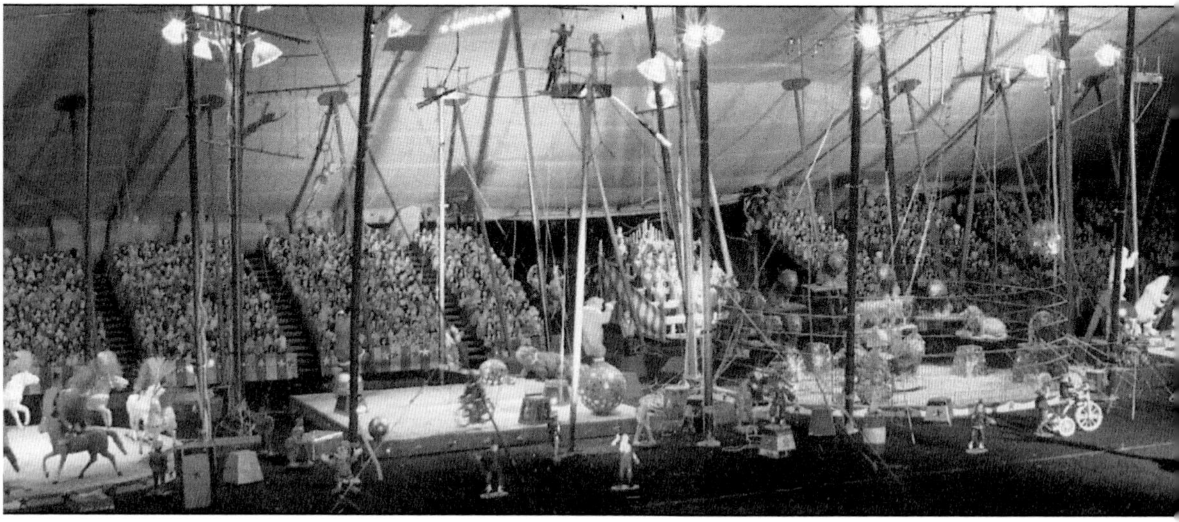

Under the Big Top was the "Greatest Show on Earth."

Earth." These large beasts were trained to move heavy equipment or to carry the tent poles with their trunks.

On the morning of the scheduled performance, most circus promoters would sponsor a parade down the main street of town. Making their appearance would be performing clowns, acrobats, various animals, trick riders on horses, and the ever-popular and noisy steam calliope.

The circus parade was such a big event for most small towns that with a written excuse from home, students would be dismissed from school to attend the public show.

Billed as "The Greatest Show on Earth," a circus generated enough events and activities to entertain everyone. Consequently, there were many sources of potential trouble for a youngster in such an exciting environment.

"I particularly remember one circus, Sells Floto, that I looked forward to attending from the first day it was scheduled in town," my father said.

"The reason for my great excitement was Tom Mix, who was the first popular cowboy. He and his horse, 'Tony', were going to be featured. My father got off from work that afternoon and took a group of boys with us. When we arrived at the circus, we all purchased cotton candy. Because I ate so much, it ruined my trip. To this day, I've never eaten cotton candy again."

While the circus specialized in magic, it was quite an amazing feat for a troupe to arrive during the morning, construct its own tent-world, then hold an afternoon and evening performance. After the last show, everything would be taken down, loaded up, and moved to another town.

The appearance of a circus in town was always an exciting event, but the excitement was unparalleled during the dark years of the Depression. The illusions it offered furnished entertainment, showmanship and ready-made thrills for a nation desperately in need of such diversions.

In today's world, with its many distractions, the circus no longer is a special event. While some large cities still play host to a circus, for those who lived during the 1930s these modern shows will never compare with the special hysteria generated by the unique individuals and wild animals who performed under "The Big Top."

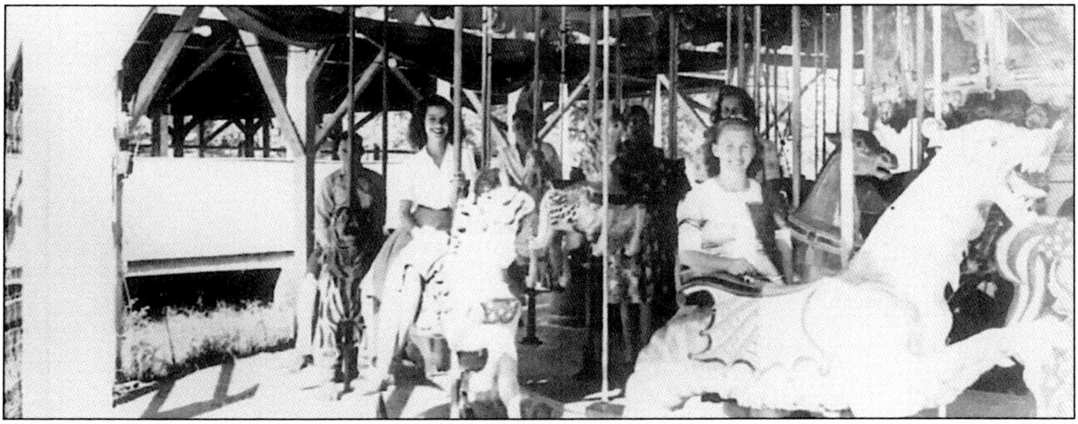

With plenty of activities, Oxford Lake was a popular spot for social events and picnics during the 1930s.

SPORTS

During the Depression, there were no organized sports for children and no playing fields provided by the city. For those interested in sports, they simply had to "make do," usually in a vacant lot within the neighborhood. If a city had a professional or semi-professional team, occasionally these fields were made available for the young players.

Since there were no organized sports, the kids from the different neighborhoods formed their own teams. In most instances, an older boy would volunteer to be the manager or coach and would contact other teams about a game. Then a time, date, and place for the game would be arranged.

Not only was there no field to play on, but the teams had no uniforms. The equipment was also inadequate, with boys using broken bats nailed together and wrapped with friction tape.

In football season, the equipment was even more pathetic. Very few players had shoulder pads or helmets and the ones that were available had been discarded by the high school.

Since the majority of the games were played within the neighborhood, it became increasingly difficult to find opponents who were not familiar rivals. Sometimes it was necessary for a team to go on the road.

"The most memorable baseball game our team played was at a Goodyear picnic," my father said. "It was held about 30 miles away and we traveled there in an open truck but since the highway wasn't paved we arrived covered in dust. The first thing we did after we got there was to go swimming, to wash off the dust, and we left dirt rings where we dived in."

"What a great picnic that turned out to be, because Goodyear provided all the free ice cream a person could eat. For a bunch of boys who rarely had even one ice cream cone, this was just too much!"

"Some members of our team ate so much they got sick and were unable to play. During the warm up, the boy who was scheduled to pitch was one of those who became sick and had to be scratched from the lineup. I'm sure he has vivid memories of that day!"

With organized sports so prevalent now, it's hard to believe young boys from that era had so few opportunities. Playing with little more than determination, these young athletes faced hardships they took in stride, always eager to play in a game they loved.

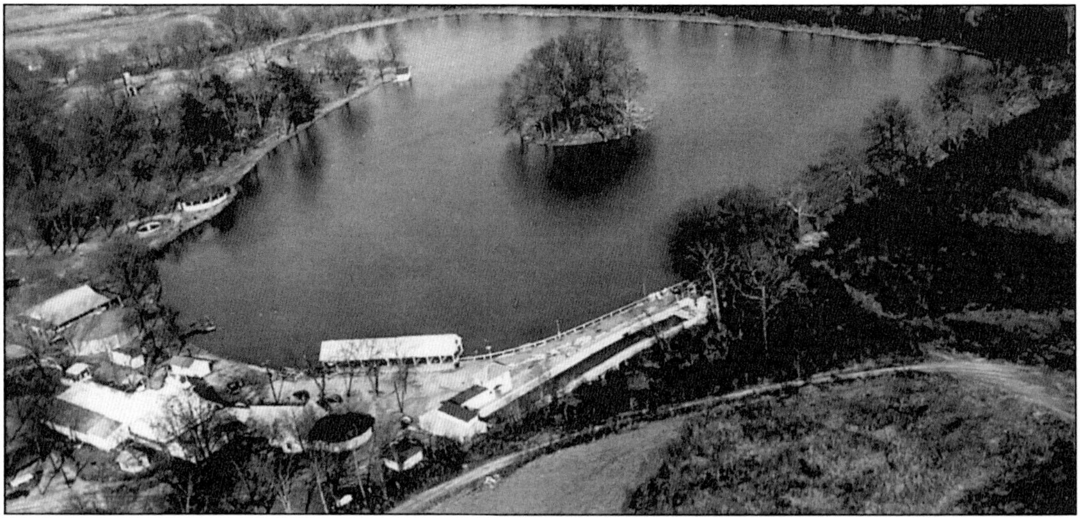

An aerial view of Oxford Lake, located near Gadsden, shows the narrow swimming pool in the foreground.

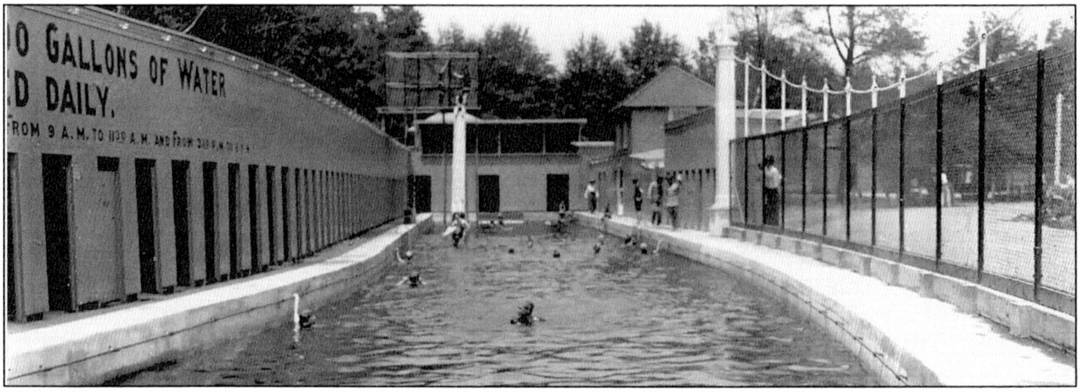

After a dusty trip, my father's baseball team dived into this pool, leaving dirt rings on the water.

Games We Played

Although surrounded by conditions of the Depression, the children of the 1930s still looked forward to spring each year. Not only did spring mean warmer weather, it represented a chance for energetic children to play games outside. While the adults sat on the porch after supper, this became the most active time for youngsters in the neighborhood.

"Hide and Seek" was a popular game of the young, as well as "Leavy-O." Similar in some ways to "Hide and Seek," "Leavy-O" was played instead with two teams guarding a circle drawn in the street. The "home" team guarded the circle while the other team would scatter and hide. If a person was caught, they were placed in the circle.

The object was for the "home" team to capture all the opposing team members and impound them in the circle. Sometimes it was possible to have two or three captives in the circle and several still running loose. If one of those who was free ran through the circle and hollered "Leavy-O!" it freed all the captives in the circle. Then the whole process would begin again.

After playing "Leavy-O" for a while, most

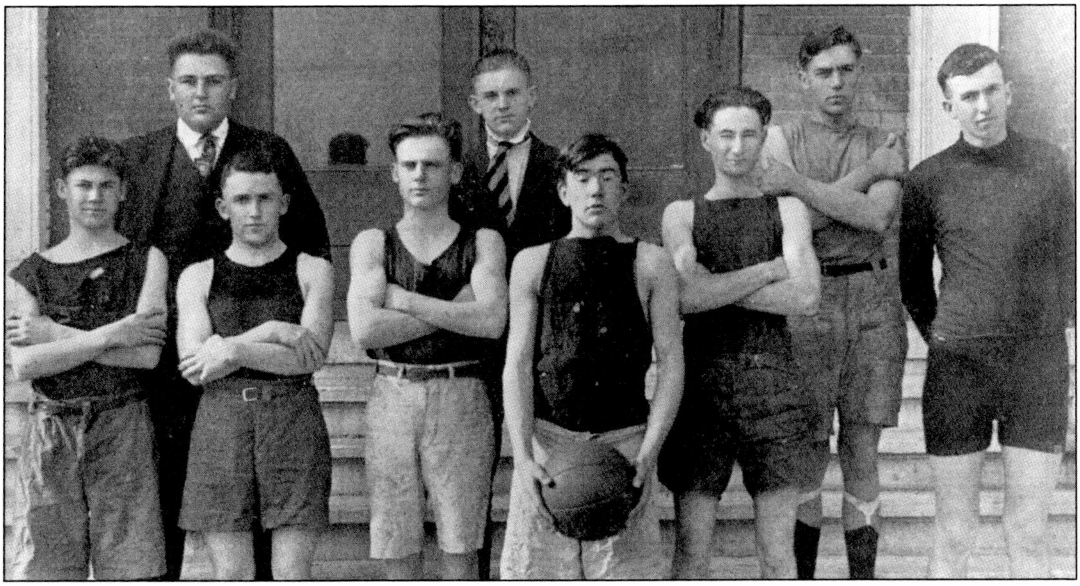

Kids from different neighborhoods would form their own teams with an older boy usually acting as coach.

boys were ready for a rest from the fast action and constant motion.

Occasionally, even a street intersection became an imaginary ball field. Here, under a street light, the young boys would engage in stick ball. This make-shift game was put into play when a broomstick turned into a bat and a tobacco sack stuffed with cotton substituted for a ball. One of the street corners would be home plate, another first base, the others second and third.

If there weren't enough boys for teams, a rotation system called "shove-up" was employed. When the batter was out, he then moved to first base and each player moved over one position in an anticlockwise motion, until the third baseman moved up into the batter's box.

"I have never heard or seen this game played anywhere except in our neighborhood," my father said.

While any number of boys could participate in stick ball, it was better when there were at least five players. This minimal lineup allowed for the all the bases to be covered and to have a pitcher and batter.

With no money and no equipment, the young boys of the Depression found ways to engage themselves in fun and sports. On spring and summer nights the air was filled with the happy sounds of kids having a good time.

Although occasionally there might be a few complaints from an "old grouch" about the noise, it was never too bad. At that time, mothers would start calling the youngest boys in to bed around 8:30 p.m. Most didn't mind, however, because they knew that the next night they would be able to do it all over again.

Marbles

In the 1930s, marbles was a game played mostly at school during recess and lunch. The school playground provided an ideal field because it was smooth and hard-packed, with no grass.

For starters, a circle would be drawn in the dirt and each player would put his marbles in the center of the ring. In order to determine the shooting order, a line would be drawn in the dirt; the person who flipped his "taw" closest to the test line was the first to shoot.

With the order of shooting determined, the players were ready to begin the game. The objective: shooting from outside, to knock any marbles out of the circle. If a marble was knocked out, it became the property of the shooter.

A person would continue to shoot until he missed, then another player had a chance. This hit-and-miss process would continue in such an order until all the marbles had been knocked out of the ring.

If the game was played for fun, each player would get his marbles back when it concluded. If, on the other hand, the game was played "for keeps," each player kept the marbles he knocked out of the ring.

Some players became so proficient at accumulating marbles in this fashion, that they ended up selling marbles back to their original owners.

"Many boys got so good at winning other's marbles they had a difficult time finding an opponent," my father said.

Like other simple amusements from the Depression era, marbles was one of the first games to make its appearance in the spring. It is also one of the oldest children's games known to man, having been played by the Romans and Egyptians before the birth of Christ.

Roller Skate Hockey

For children with few opportunities to play organized sports, roller skate hockey was an invented game played in one particular neighborhood during the 1930s. While most of the boys in the neighborhood owned skates, their game was a unique version of the sport. Since none of them had ever seen a live hockey match, they simply played by their own set of rules.

The playing field chosen by these neighborhood athletes was one block of a public street. It was paved with concrete, which made the skating easier, but old streetcar tracks in the middle of the pavement created natural hazards.

To start the game, a puck was placed in the middle of the block. Next, to put the puck in play, opposing team members would touch their sticks together three times and, on the third time, hit the puck. This meant the game was on!

Similar to professional hockey teams, each team had a goal; but, unlike the major leagues, these teams' goals didn't have a net. Each one would simply try to knock the puck across a line at the end of the block.

Reflecting the improvised attitude toward the sport, the boy's hockey sticks were sawed-off broomsticks and the puck was a small Pet Milk can. After many licks the can became dented and disfigured with many sharp points, and turned into a lethal weapon if it caught a player on the shin.

Another hazard was being rapped on the shins by the opponent's broomstick. Unlike pro hockey players, these young boys had no protective equipment to protect them from injuries. Many times a hockey stick would find its way into a pair of the opponent's skates and down he'd go! Such rough-and-tumble antics resulted in numerous skinned knees.

"Looking back, I'm amazed no one was seriously injured in this youthful pastime," my father said.

Roller skate hockey was a tough and fast-moving game for young boys. Although at the end of the day all the players went home tired, some were bruised and bleeding, while others received torn clothing as a reward for their participation in this neighborhood sport.

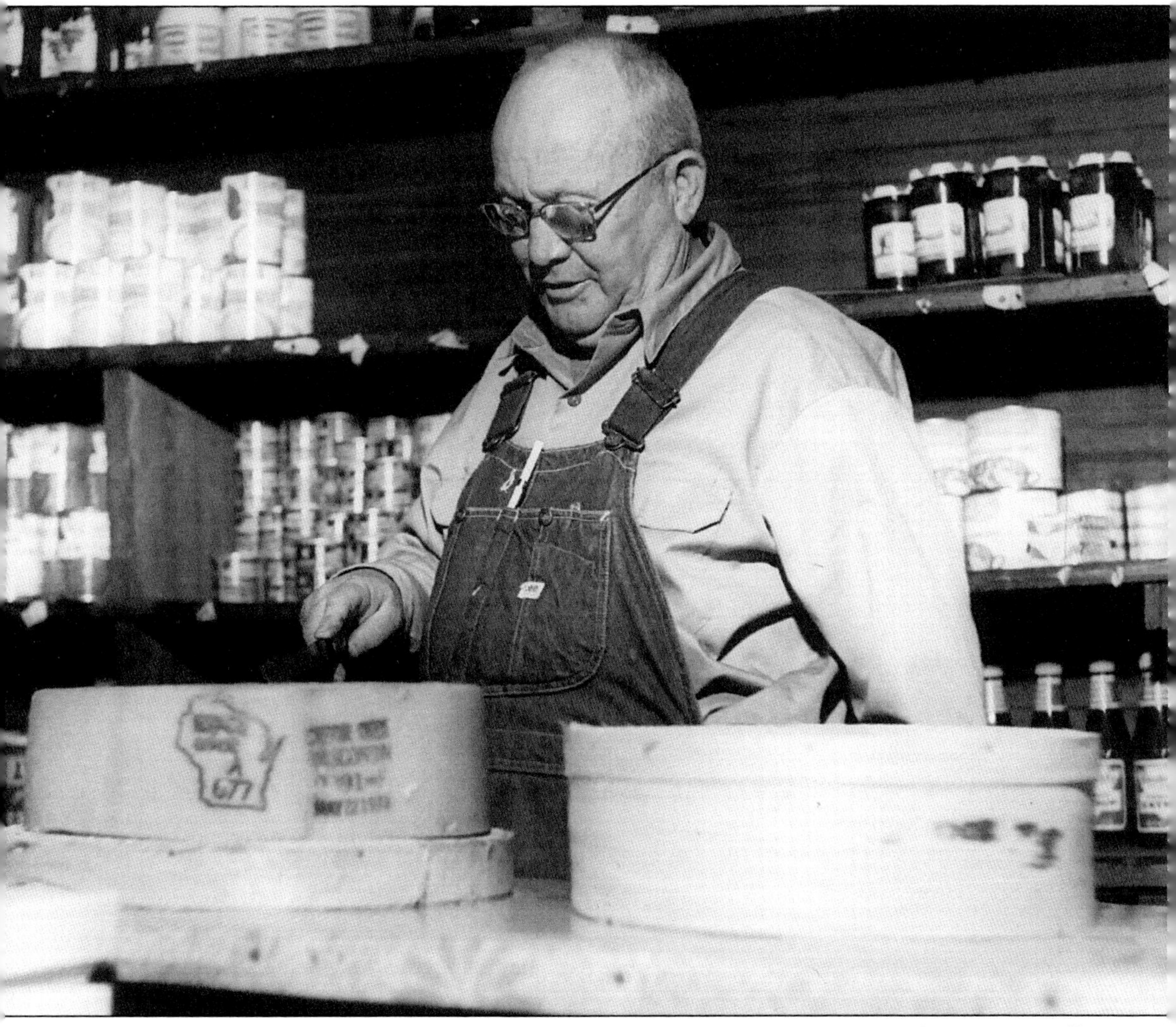

In earlier times, cheese was not kept refrigerated. The store owner pictured here cuts off a piece of "hoop cheese."

VISITING IN THE COUNTRY

Most people who lived in the city during the 1930s had relatives in the country. When school was out for the summer, one of the things city children looked forward to was a visit to their relative's farm.

Life on a farm was practically all work, but there was an interlude during the summer when all the crops had been cultivated and laid-by. This was an excellent time to visit because it presented the only opportunity farmers had to fool with city relatives who knew nothing about farming.

In those days, farms were a family operation and covered about 40 acres. While these farms were almost self-sufficient, money was needed for clothes and some grocery items such as coffee, sugar, and flour.

To purchase the few necessities required for his operation, each farmer had to have a cash crop. For people in the South, this meant cotton. In the fall of the year, after the cotton was picked, ginned, and sold, the farmer then went to town and

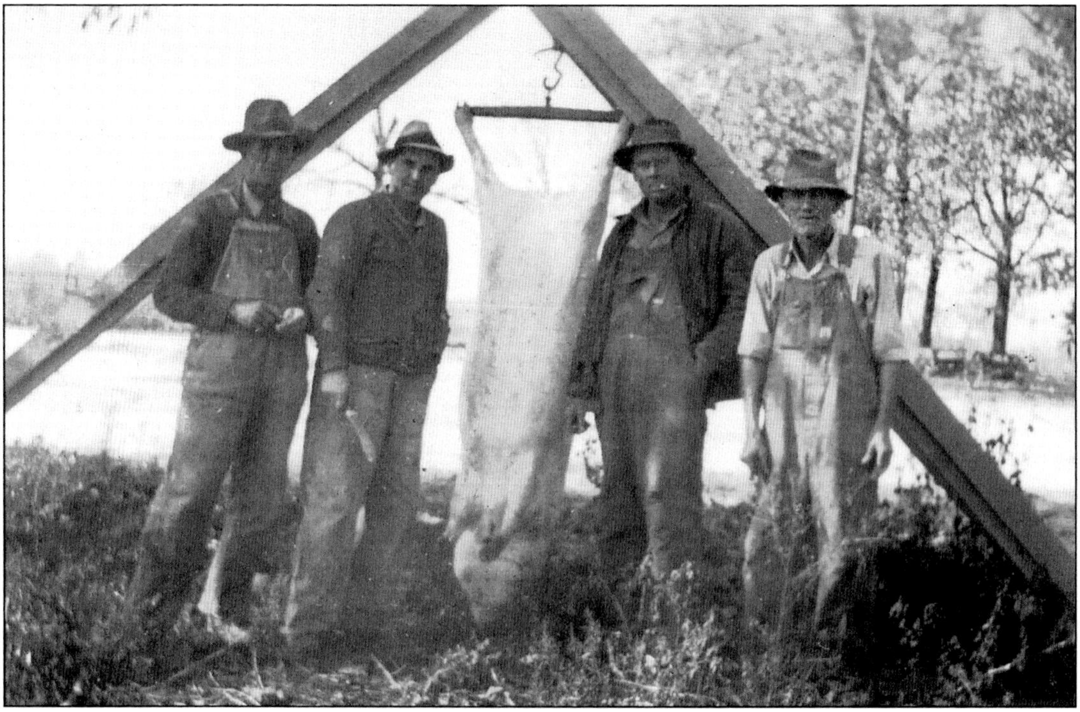

A "hog killin'" in the country can be seen in the photograph above.

purchased whatever was needed to carry him through the winter.

My father, who often visited his relatives in the country, says he can still picture his uncle's farm as it existed over 60 years ago.

"On one side of his house he had a field planted in either cotton or corn. Then, across the road, was a pasture and barn. Next to the barn, another field was planted in more cotton or corn. For soil preservation, these crops were rotated every year."

On the other side of his uncle's farmhouse was a garden with a fence around it. This fence was necessary because of an abundance of rabbits that seemed to think the garden was planted exclusively for their benefit. For the farmer though, the garden not only supplied fresh vegetables in season, but also provided a supply of produce for canning purposes.

Behind the main house another field was sown in hay, with a small portion set aside for a watermelon patch. Removed from this field, in a wooded area, sat the hog pen.

Animals and chickens played important roles on the farm. Every farm had a cow to supply milk and butter and chickens to provide meat and eggs. Besides these animals, every farmer usually kept one or two hogs to be fattened for slaughter when the weather turned cold. After the slaughter, since there was no way to keep the meat refrigerated, it was "salted down" and placed in a wooden meat box until needed.

An extremely stubborn animal, a mule was used for plowing and transportation—to bring corn, cotton, and hay from the fields, to take cotton to the gin, and to transport the bales of cotton to town to be sold. Whenever the roads were impassable for an automobile, a mule and wagon offered the only transportation to the store, grist mill, or community picnics. The syrup mill was also a favorite destination, because it provided a glimpse into the process of turning sorghum cane into sweet sorghum syrup.

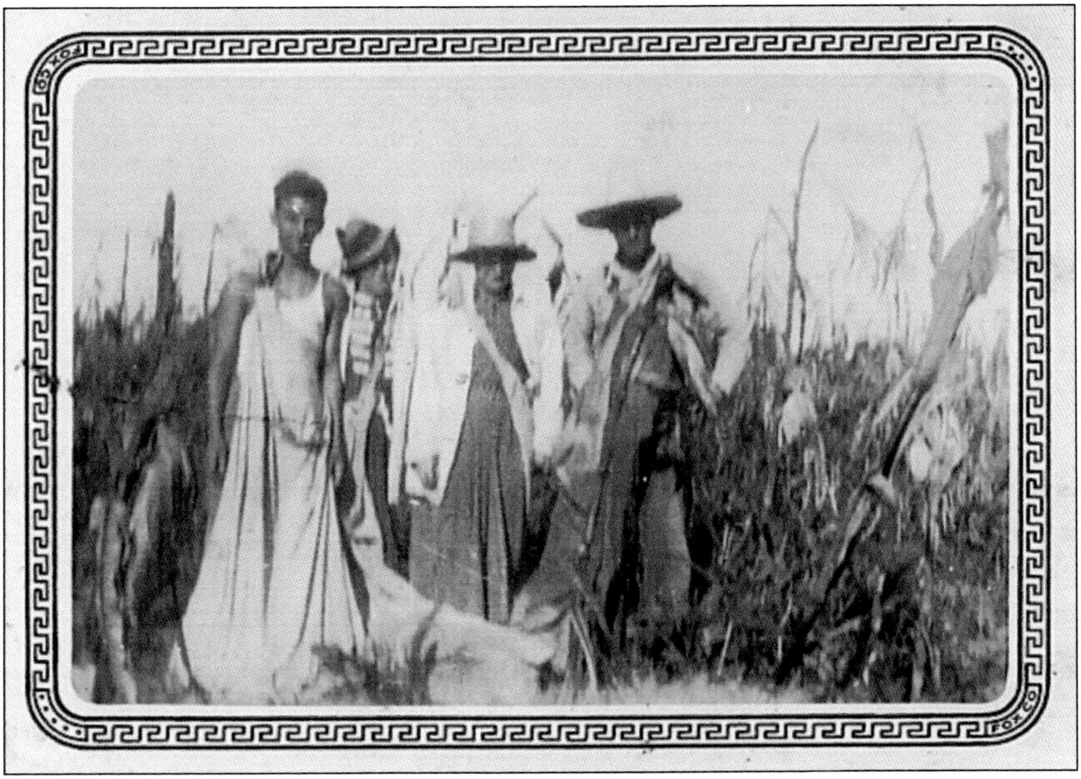

My father, at left with the cotton picking sack, is pictured here during one of his visits to the country.

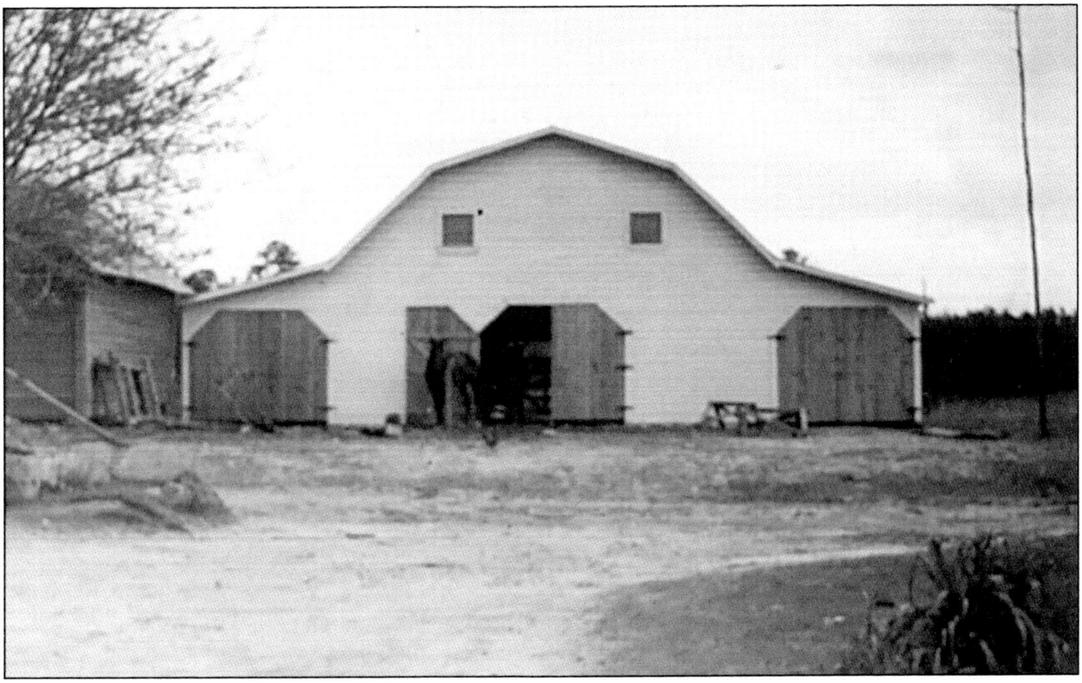

The barn of my father's uncle as it existed over 60 years ago.

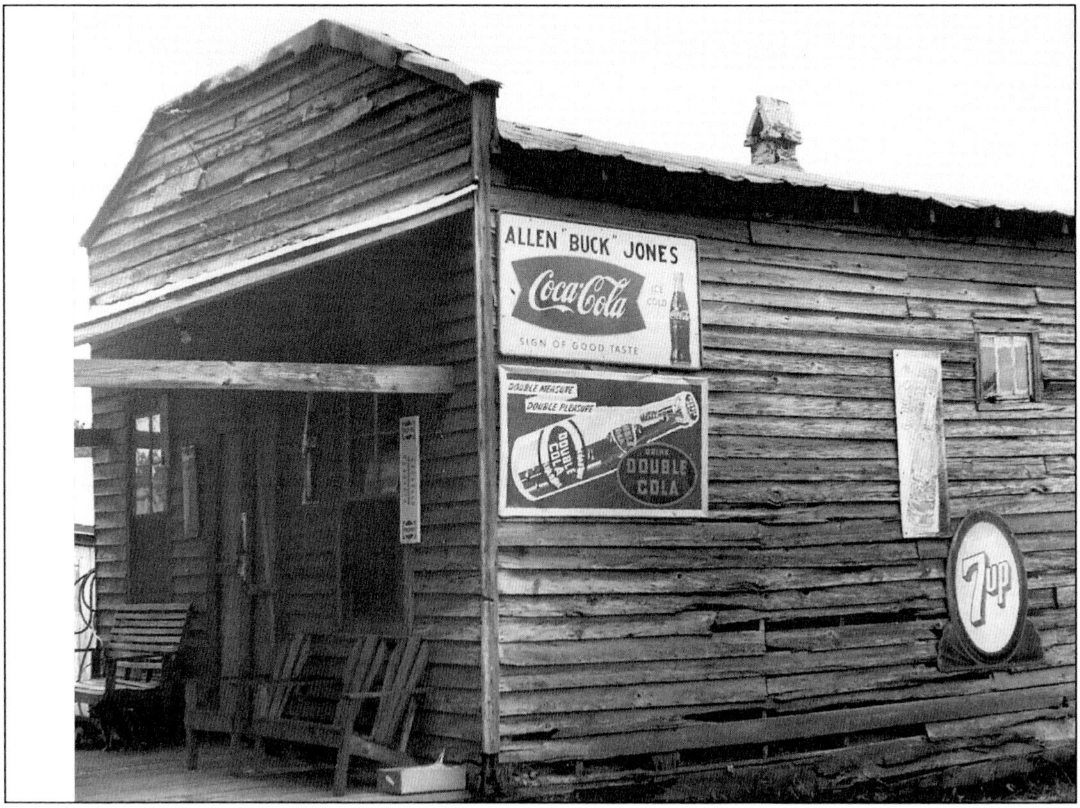

The old country store was a focal point for the rural community in the country.

One memorable experience of these country visits for my father was riding in a wagon.

"My uncle had two mules, one named 'John' and the other 'Rodie.' It was quite a treat when he would hitch the mules to the wagon and I would sit by him on the seat, holding the reins as we traveled down the road."

Another pleasurable aspect of these holidays that still stands out in his mind were the big country meals, especially breakfast.

"Some mornings we'd be served a big platter of scrambled eggs, sausage or country ham, sorghum, fresh churned butter, biscuits and coffee. Other mornings we might have fried chicken, white milk gravy, biscuits and coffee."

Today, most—if not all—of these self-sufficient country farms are gone, a victim of "progress" and the ever-increasing cost of running a small family operation. While the family farm as it existed in the 1930s has now faded into obscurity, those long, lazy summer days visiting country relatives remain distinct in the memory of those who lived during that era.

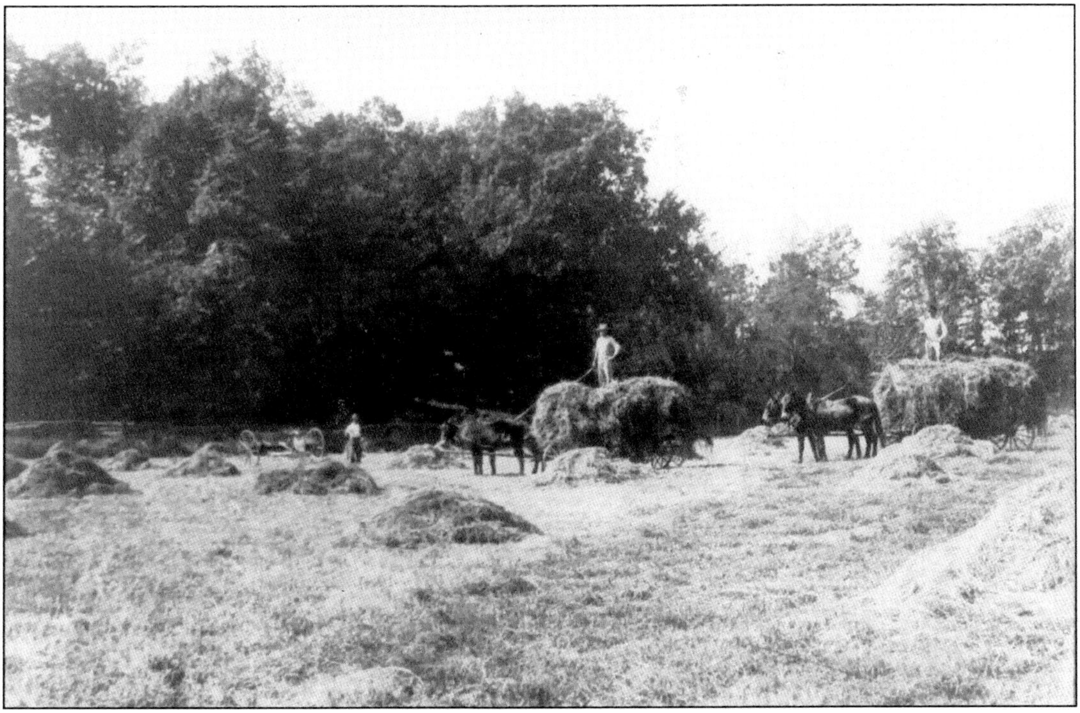

These people are loading hay to store in the barn.

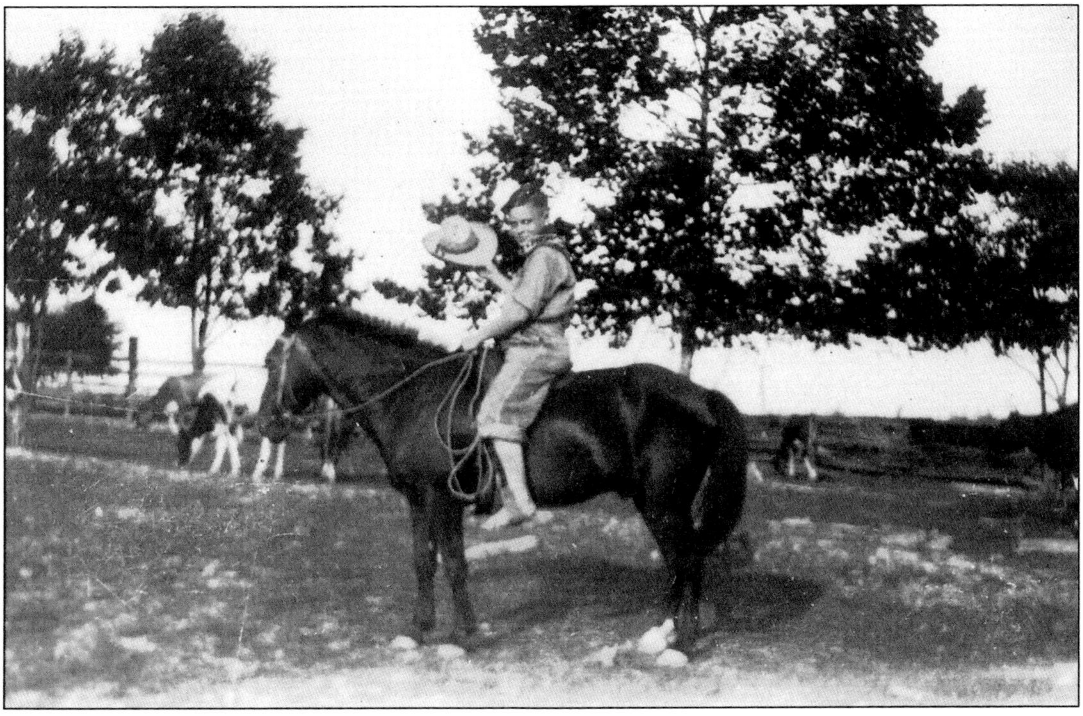

My father's cousin, James, on "Tar Baby" in the 1930s.

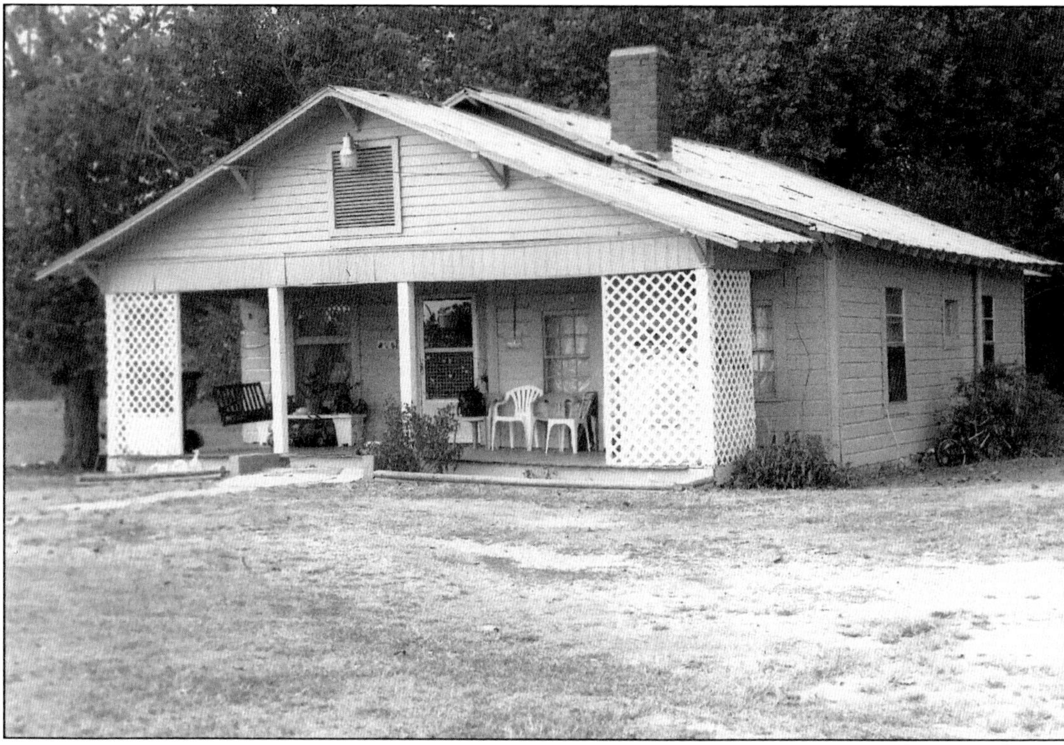

During the Depression, my father would stay in this house when he visited his aunt, uncle, and cousin.

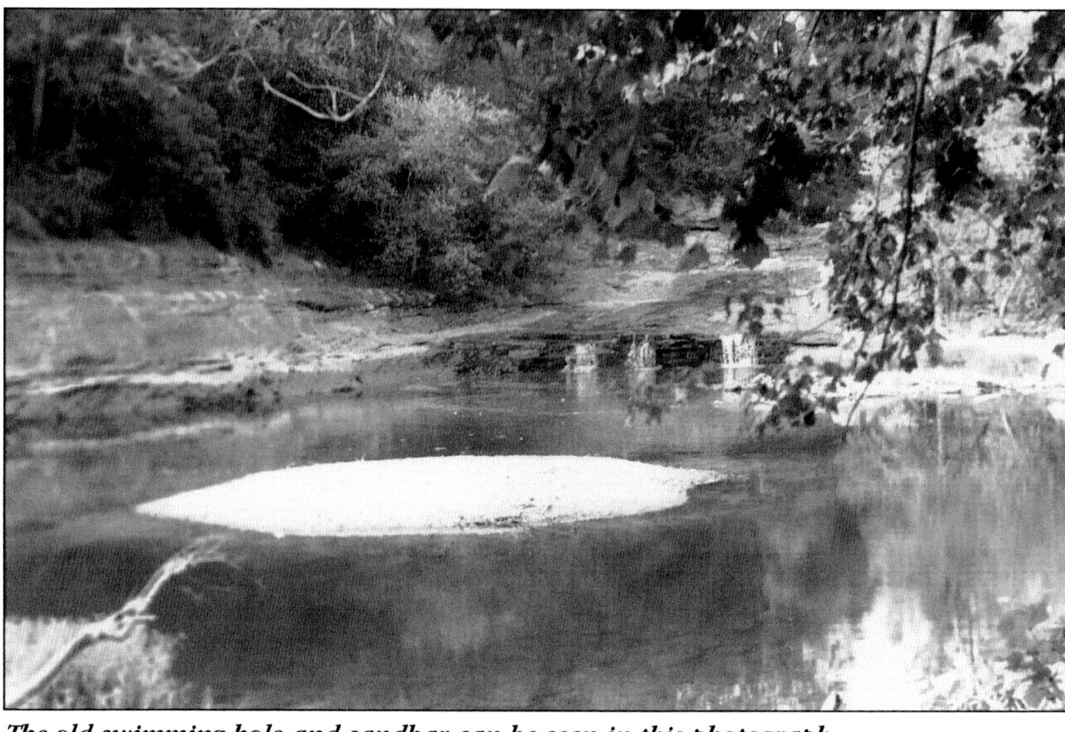

The old swimming hole and sandbar can be seen in this photograph.

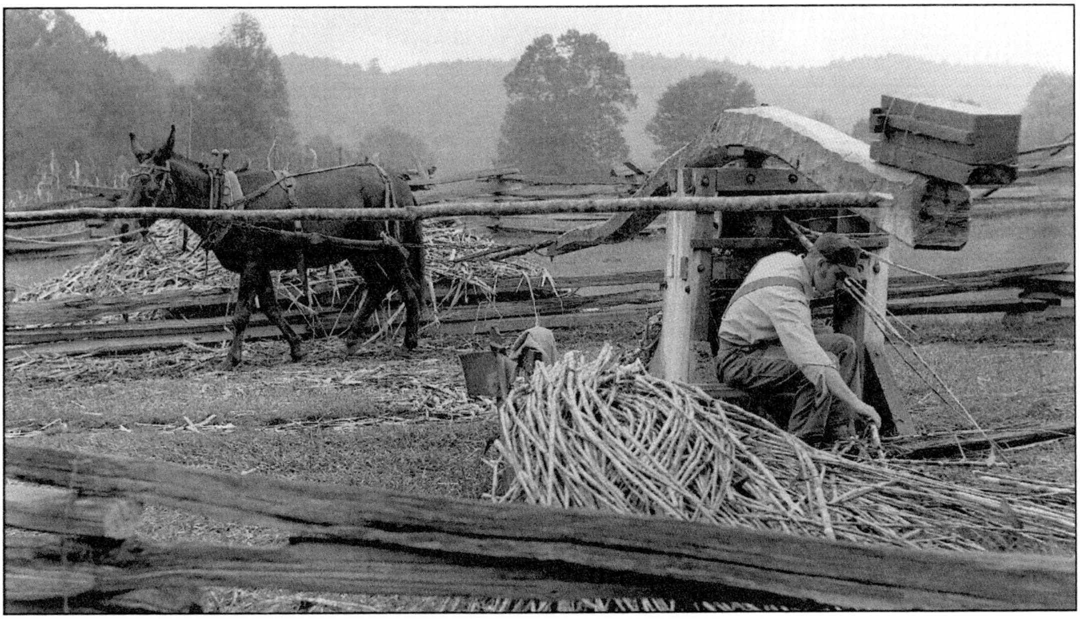

The first part of sorghum making is to extract the juice from the raw cane. A mule walking around the cane press supplies the power to turn the rollers in the press.

Making Sorghum

When fall arrives each year, those with a rural background are reminded of how this season once affected their lives. Fall on a Southern farm was a busy season: a time of picking cotton, gathering corn, and making molasses—commonly called "sogum surp."

Each farm, in addition to its corn and cotton crop, usually had a small plot set aside for a cane patch. The cane was planted in the spring and ripened in the fall, at which time it was stripped, cut, loaded on the wagon and taken to the mill.

The processing of the sorghum was a community affair, with each community having its own mill and its own expert in the making of sorghum.

Gathering at the mill served both a useful and a social purpose; the people stood around while the sorghum was cooking and enjoyed the fellowship of their neighbors.

First, the stripped cane would be fed into the rollers of the mill. The mule, walking around in a circle, supplied the power to turn the rollers.

As the rollers turned, juice was squeezed from the cane and collected in buckets. From the bucket, the juice would then be strained into the cooker over the fire. This cooker was made with a number of partitions called baffles.

The juice slowly moved from one baffle to another, gradually thickening as it traveled, until it reached the last baffle—where it was taken out as sorghum. During this time, more juice was constantly added to keep the process going and it was skimmed regularly to make the syrup clear.

With the sorghum made, it was poured into syrup buckets to be taken home. Usually the owner of the mill was paid for his labors by the collection of a toll, a certain percentage of the sorghum going to him in lieu of cash.

Many people have fond memories of cold winter mornings when they sat down to a breakfast of scrambled eggs, country ham, hot biscuits, fresh churned butter, and sorghum syrup.

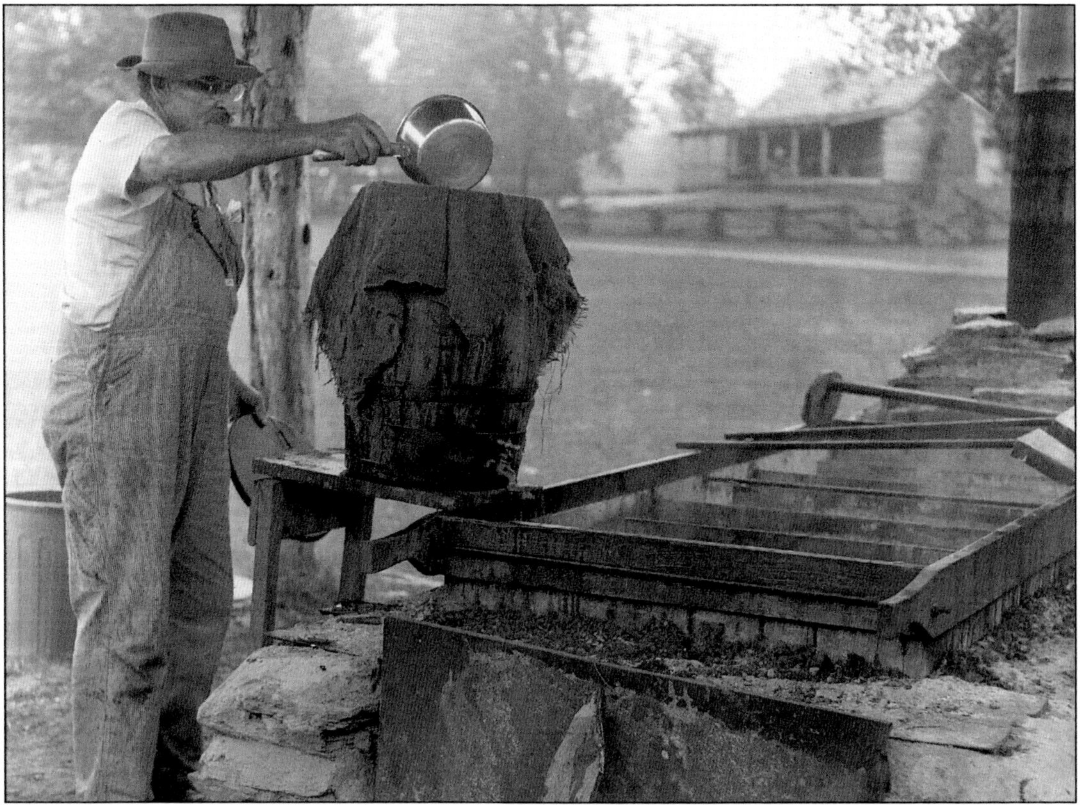

In sorghum making, the juice is strained before cooking.

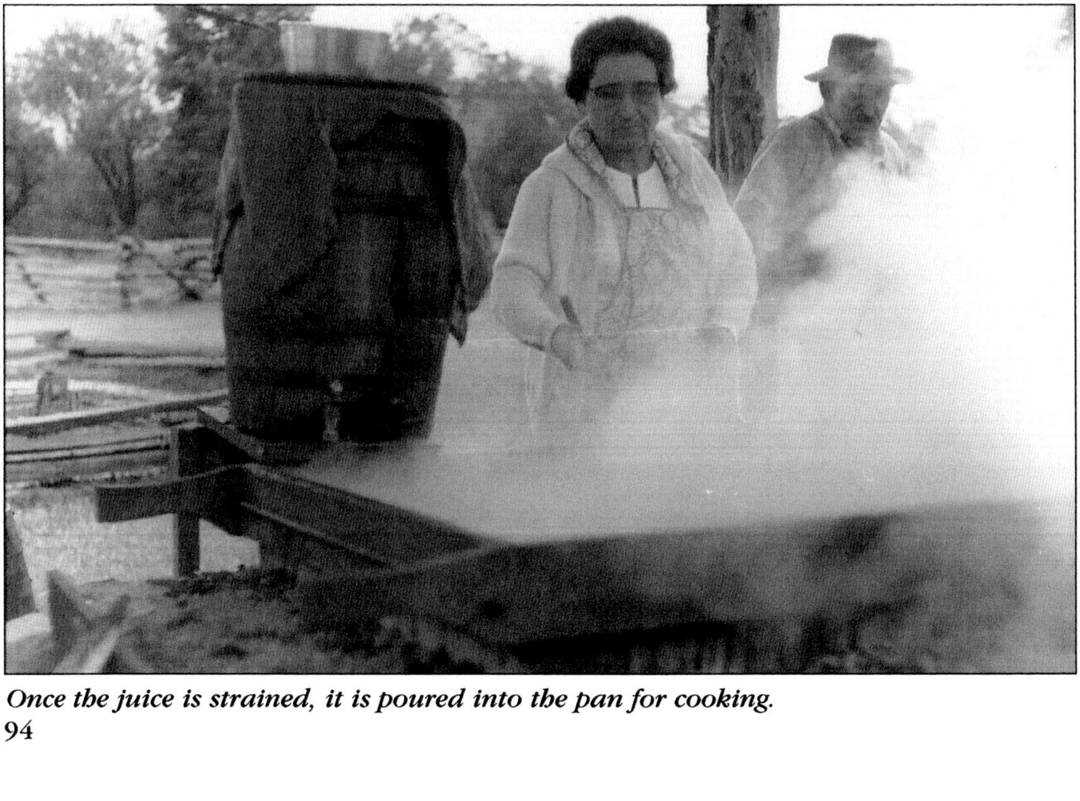

Once the juice is strained, it is poured into the pan for cooking.

Conclusion

The decade of the 1930s, the period of years that spanned the Great Depression, was an unprecedented time in the history of America. Never before or since has there been such uncertainty, confusion and hopelessness in the life of the average citizen of this country.

For those who did not live during the 1930s, if this book has shed new light on such dark days and on the people who lived through the Great Depression, it has served its purpose. May they draw inspiration from the sacrifice of an earlier generation.

On the other hand, I hope that this book has brought back some pleasant memories of a past generation, a vanished way of life, for those individuals who were alive when the stock market crashed in 1929, when "Hoovervilles" were a common sight on the outskirts of most cities, and when F.D.R. brokered his "New Deal" with America.

The Great Depression was an unforgettable experience for those who lived through it. For those who were not alive, mere words can never fully describe the difficulties of an entire nation struggling to survive collapse against almost unsurmountable odds. Yet through hard work, determination, and faith in God—the nation and her people survived.

END NOTES

1. Broadman, Fan W., Jr. *The Thirties.* New York: Henry Z. Walck, Inc., 1967.

2. Wecter, Dixon. *Age of the Great Depression.* New York: The Macmillan Company, 1941 (p. 8).

3. Brogan, Dennis. *The Era of Franklin D. Roosevelt.* New York: U.S. Publishers Association, Inc., 1950.

4. Hurley, Jack F. *Portrait of A Decade.* Baton Rouge: Louisiana State Press, 1972.

5. Wecter, Dixon. *Age of the Great Depression.* New York: The Macmillan Company, 1941.